RĀMA

His Historicity, Mandir and Setu

Evidence of Literature, Archaeology and Other Sciences

RĀMA

His Historicity, Mandir and Setu

Evidence of Literature, Archaeology and Other Sciences

B.B. LAL

Aryan Books International
New Delhi

RĀMA: HIS HISTORICITY, MANDIR AND SETU

ISBN: 978-81-7305-345-0

First Hardback Edition Published

in **2019** by:

Aryan Books International

Pooja Apartments, 4B, Ansari Road, New Delhi-110 002 (India)

Tel.: 23287589, 23255799; Fax: 91-11-23270385

E-mail: aryanbooks@gmail.com

www.aryanbooks.com

Computer Typeset and Printed in India by

ABI Prints & Publishing Co., New Delhi.

Dedicated to my countrymen
who have always been worshippers
of the truth and even today live by the ideal

"Satyameva Jayate"

Preface

This booklet seeks to present archaeological facts, nothing but hard facts, in regard to the three topics which have become, as it were, the 'talk of the day', viz.: (i) 'Was Rāma a figment of the imagination of a poet called Vālmīki, or is there any evidence to suggest that he may have been a historical figure?'; (ii) 'Was there a temple in the Janma-Bhūmi area at Ayodhyā, prior to the construction of the Babari Masjid?'; and (iii) 'What are the "credentials" of the Rāma Setu'?

Of late I have been busy finalizing my next book, *How Deep are the Roots of Indian Civilization? Archaeology Answers.* But in the midst of this schedule, for more than a month now I have also been attending to calls from television channels, print media and a number of eminent individuals asking for my views on the above-mentioned topics. In fact, the *Sahara Samaya* channel, not finding me in Delhi, got hold of me at Fursatganj (Raibareli) where my wife and I were spending some quiet time with our eldest son and daughter-in-law. This channel insisted on interviewing me over the telephone on September 15 and aired the same for its listeners. The *NDTV*, I was told, wanted me to participate in a debate on the Rāma Setu issue around the same time, but could not get me since I was away. However, a very senior editor of the *India Today* had a long telephonic conversation with me on the subject and published some of my views in its Special Issue dated October 1, 2007.

Since the telephone still keeps on ringing, I thought it was better for me to write out a small booklet on the above-mentioned issues so that all those who are interested in knowing the archaeological and allied evidence are not deprived of it.

With these few words, I have the pleasure of placing this booklet in the hands of inquisitive readers, hoping that they would find it of some interest.

Vijaya Dashami
October 21, 2007

B.B. Lal

Contents

Acknowledgements

In securing illustrations and some data for this booklet many colleagues and friends have lent their helping hands. They include Dr. J.P. Joshi, Professor O.P. Tandon, Professor Vidula Jayaswal, Dr. D.P. Sharma, Professor Makkhan Lal, Dr. B.R. Mani, Dr. D.V. Sharma, Dr. Daljeet, Dr. Virajanand Daivakarni, Shri S.K. Sharma, Shri Vishnu Kant and my granddaughter, Anjali. To all of them I am most grateful. I am most grateful to Professor Monica Smith of UCLA who has helped me in obtaining permission from the Los Angeles County Museum of Art to reproduce the figure of Rāma, used on the cover. My son, Rajesh, has gone through the draft and has offered some very useful suggestions; though it would be a formality to thank him, I think I must do that.

In order to keep the price-tag down, I have decided not to accept any royalty from the publisher. More importantly, however, the publisher himself, Shri Vikas Arya, has volunteered to sell this book on a no-profit-no-loss basis, for which I am indeed greatly beholden to him.

List of Illustrations

However, in this long trench and in other smaller ones too ancient remains were duly met with. (Courtesy ASI)

1.8 Bharadvāja Āśrama: A view of another trench. In it two successive structures were met with in the upper levels. Lower down there were no structures, but only deposits of sandy loam, which yielded sporadically sherds of the Northern Black Polished Ware as well as lumps of clay with reed-marks. (Courtesy ASI)

1.9 Bharadvāja Āśrama: A lump of clay with reed-marks, suggesting the presence of wattle-and-daub huts. (Courtesy ASI)

1.10 Kauśāmbī: A 2nd-1st century BCE terracotta. It shows Rāvaṇa carrying away Sītā, after abducting her. She drops down her ornaments in the hope that these might be picked up by someone, which would help in tracing her whereabouts. This depiction tallies very well with the description in the *Rāmāyaṇa* of Vālmīki. (Courtesy Allahabad Museum)

1.11 A terracotta figure currently lodged in the Los Angeles County Museum of Art, USA, but believed to have come from Nachāra Kherā in Haryana. It portrays Rāma whose name is also inscribed, in Brāhmī characters of the 3rd century CE. (Courtesy LACMA)

1.12 Nachāra Kherā, Haryana: A terracotta plaque depicting a scene from the *Rāmāyaṇa.* It is inscribed in Brāhmī characters of the 4th century CE. (Courtesy Haryānā Prāntīya Purātattva Saṁgrahālaya (HPPS), Gurukula, Jhajjar, Haryana.

1.13 Another terracotta panel from Nachāra Kherā, ascribable to the 4th century CE. Though broken, it still shows Rāma (upper part broken), Lakṣmaṇa and Sītā, with a deer attempting to run away. The scene tallies with the relevant part of the *Rāmāyaṇa* text. (Courtesy HPPS, Jhajjar)

1.14 A terracotta panel from Jind, Haryana. It bears an inscription in Brāhmī characters of the 4th century CE,

CHAPTER I

Was Rāma a Real-life Person or Mythical?

A. INTRODUCTORY

The recent controversy about the Rāma Setu has offered an opportunity to certain individuals to question even the historicity of Rāma. They would rather like to relegate him to the realm of myth. Their approach is quite ingenious. If the very existence of Rāma as a real-life person is denied, the question of there having been a Setu associated with him automatically does not arise. In this context, one cannot help quoting the learned Chief Minister of Tamil Nadu who recently raised two very interesting questions, namely "Who is this Rāma?" and "From which engineering college did he graduate?" (The Hindustan Times, Lucknow edn., September 19, 2007, p. 7.) **But perhaps this present-day ruler of Tamil Nadu is unaware of the fact that in an inscription issued by one of his predecessors ruling the same land more than 1200 years ago, namely Nandivarman, there are two very clear references to Rāma. The inscription is the well known Kāśākuḍī plate inscription dated to 752-53 CE. In it (Verse 22) one of the predecessors of Nandivarman, namely Narasiṁhavarman, is mentioned as having 'surpassed the glory of the valour of Rāma by (his) conquest of Laṅka'. Again (in Verse 29), Nandivarman himself is stated to 'resemble Rāma in archery.'** Indeed, the exploits of Rāma had been mentioned even much earlier, namely in the earliest part of the *Sangama* literature of Tamil Nadu, dating back to a couple of centuries before the beginning of the Common (Christian) Era. A verse in the *Puranānūru* collection states that when Rāvaṇa, after abducting Sītā, was carrying her away, she dropped down her ornaments so that these may lead to her being traced out. This very theme forms the subject-matter of a terracotta representation ascribable to the 2nd-1st century BCE (Fig. 1.10).

Those who already have a fixed mind-set are welcome to continue with it, but there are thousands of others who would like to know some facts and figures about this issue. For their sake, therefore, it is proposed to present in this chapter first the life-story of Rāma as given in Indian literature – not only Brāhmaṇical but also Buddhist and Jain. Thereafter, a brief presentation will be made of Rāmāyaṇic literature in other Asian countries.

Some time back I had undertaken a project called 'Archaeology of the Rāmāyaṇa Sites', under which five sites associated with the story were excavated. A brief summary of these excavations will thus be presented. This will be followed by the portrayal of the life of Rāma in various art-media, such as terracottas, stone sculptures and paintings, both in India and abroad. Finally, an overview of the entire evidence will be presented on the basis of which the readers would be in a position to draw their own conclusions.

B. RĀMA'S LIFE-STORY IN LITERATURE

As stated earlier, we shall deal here, though briefly, with the evidence regarding the life of Rāma, as available in Brāhmaṇical, Buddhist and Jain literature, both in India and abroad.

1. The *Rāmāyaṇa* of Vālmīki

We begin our enquiry with a look at the *Rāmāyaṇa* of Vālmīki, which is the basic source of the story of Rāma. While opinions slightly vary in respect of its antiquity, it is generally held by most scholars that, though there may have been an earlier beginning in the form of an orally sung ballad, the written version of this *Rāmāyaṇa* (there are many other *Rāmāyaṇa*s to which we shall refer shortly) may have commenced around the 3rd century BCE. The text, as available to us now, has about 24,000 *śloka*s (verses) and is divided into seven *Kāṇḍa*s (Cantos), namely *Bāla, Ayodhyā, Araṇya, Kiṣkindhā, Sundara, Yuddha,* and *Uttara Kāṇḍa*s. At the same time, it is also held that the first and last-named *Kāṇḍa*s are later additions, there being originally only five. However, along with these two *Kāṇḍa*s, the entire text appears to have been completed by the end of the third century CE.

Although the life-story of Rāma is fairly well known, it may nevertheless be worth while to refresh our memory, in as few words as possible. Daśaratha, the king of the Kosala dynasty, with the capital at Ayodhyā, had three wives, named Kauśilyā, Sumitrā and Kaikeyī. The first-named gave birth to Rāma, the second to Lakṣmaṇa and Śatrughna and the last one to Bharata. When Daśaratha grew old he wanted to anoint his eldest son, Rāma, as the king. But Kaikeyī, to whom Daśaratha had given two boons on an earlier occasion, demanded that her son, Bharata, be appointed the king and Rāma be sent away on an exile for fourteen years. Daśaratha had to yield, and Rāma, along with his wife, Sītā, and brother, Lakṣmaṇa, left Ayodhyā. In their southward journey, they crossed the Gaṅgā at Śṛiṅgaverapura, stopped overnight at the *Āśrama* of sage Bharadvāja, and reached Chitrakūṭa where they stayed for quite some time. It was here that Bharata came to meet Rāma and request him to return to Ayodhyā and take over the reigns of the government. Rāma did not accede to Bharata's request, but gave the latter his *pādukā*s (sandals) as his symbol and asked the latter to return home and rule on his behalf. After spending some time at Chitrakūṭa, the trio went southwards and stayed Pañchavaṭī, near Nashik. Here, one day Rāvaṇa came in the guise of a mendicant and abducted Sītā. Naturally aggrieved, Rāma, along with Lakṣmaṇa, set out in search of Sītā. On their way southwards, they met

Sugrīva and Hanumān who helped the former in their mission. It was discovered that Sītā had been abducted by Rāvaṇa, king of Laṅkā. Arrangements were made to bridge the relevant parts of the shallow sea between mainland India and Laṅkā and Rāma's army crossed over to Laṅkā. Finally, Rāvaṇa was killed and Sītā rescued. After the victory, Rāma, Sītā and Lakṣmaṇa returned to Ayodhyā and Rāma was coronated as the king.

In the course of time, the story of Rāma became so popular that it was rendered into various languages not only in India but also abroad, and these range in date from after the time of Vālmīki's *Rāmāyaṇa* right up to the 20th century. Though almost every part of the country abounds in Rāmāyaṇic narrations, we give here just a few examples, respectively from the east, west, north and south.

2. In West Bengal and Bangladesh

There are many references to Rāma in early inscriptions, such as in the Khalimpur copper-plate grant of Dharmapāla (eighth century CE), and in sculptures, for example in the Paharpur temple of the same century. However, the earliest *Rāmāyaṇa* in Bengali language is that of Kṛittivāsa who, according most scholars, was born in 1389 CE. While using the *Rāmāyaṇa* of Vālmīki as his base, Kṛittivāsa made many additions of his own. Anyway, this version is highly popular and is read with great veneration in Bengali households. There are scores of other *Rāmāyaṇa*s in the Bengali language, such as the *Adbhuta Rāmāyaṇa* of Kailash Basu (1586 CE), and another *Adbhuta Rāmāyaṇa*, this time of Adbhutāchārya (seventeenth century CE). In this context, special mention must be made of a poetess named Chandravatī, also of the seventeenth century, who narrated the Rāmāyaṇa story through inspiring folk songs.

3. In Gujarat

The earliest known work in Gujarat relating to the Rāmāyaṇa story seems to be the *Bhaṭṭi Kāvya*, assignable to sixth century CE. Its authorship is attributed to Bhatṛihari, who used examples from the story of Ṛāma to illustrate the rules of Sanskrit grammar. What a novel idea! A play called *Dūtāṅgada* was written by Subhaṭa in the thirteenth century. It narrated the episode of Aṅgada, a well known figure in the Rāmāyaṇa story, and was meant to be staged on the occasion of the Spring Festival. Another noteworthy work of the same century is *Ullāgharāghava,* by Someśvara. It follows the sequence of events given in the *Rāmāyaṇa* of Vālmīki.

In the Gujarati language, the story of Rāma seems to have been rendered for the first time in the fourteenth century. It is encapsulated in the songs known as *Rāmārlīlā-nā-pado,* composed by Āśait. In the following century came up Bhālana whose *Rāma-vivāha* deserves mention. Indeed, once the ball was set rolling there came up many works, well over fifty, in the Gujarati language on the *Rāmāyaṇa* theme. These deal with either the entire story or a given part thereof. And what is interesting is that the tradition has been carried down right up to the twentieth century. In this context, mention may be made of the *Rāmāyaṇa* of Girdhardāsa, written in the nineteenth century, which perhaps is the most popular one.

4. In Uttar Pradesh

The life of Rāma began in Uttar Pradesh wherein he was born at Ayodhyā. It is, therefore, but natural that his life-story is very much alive in that state. It would not be an exaggeration to say that there would hardly be any Hindu household in Uttar Pradesh which does not keep with veneration a copy of the *Rāmacharitamānasa* of the saint-poet Tulasīdāsa. In fact, it is a common practice in Uttar Pradesh to do *akhaṇḍa-pāṭha* (incessant recital) of the *Rāmacharitamānasa,* which generally takes more than a day. While there is some debate about the date of birth of Tulasīdāsa, it is well recorded that he passed away in 1623 CE.

Akbar, the renowned Mughal ruler of India (1556-1605 CE), was a liberal and took interest in Hinduism as well.

Accordingly, he directed Badauni to translate the *Rāmāyaṇa* in Persian. Writes Badauni:

> In the month of Jamada'l-Awwal of the year 997 [A.H.] I finished the translation of the *Rāmāyaṇa* which has taken me four years. I wrote it all in couplets and brought it to the Emperor.

Akbar's liberalism can be adjudged from another fact, namely that he issued gold and silver coins bearing the figures of Rāma and Sītā and inscribed with the legend *Rāma Siya* (Fig. 1.1).

While there were many more poets in Uttar Pradesh during the mediaeval times whose works deal with the theme of Rāma's life, I would like to draw attention to the fact that even in the 20th century the theme continued to attract poetic genius. Thus, whereas the *Rāmacharitamānasa* of Tulasīdāsa was in Avadhī, a local language of eastern Uttar Pradesh, the 20th century poets used Hindī (technically known as the Khaḍī Bolī). In this context special mention may be made of the *Rāmāyaṇa* by Radhey Shyama and *Sāketa* by Maithili Sharana Gupta.

The Rāmāyaṇa theme attracted the attention of temple-builders as well, who portrayed in stone excellent sculptures depicting the Rāmāyaṇa story. To these we shall refer a little later.

Fig. 1.1. A coin issued by Akbar, portraying Rāma and Sītā along with their names.

5. In Karnataka

After the abduction of Sītā at Pañchavaṭī, Rāma and Lakṣmaṇa started southwards in her search. In due course of time they reached Kiṣkindhā where they met Hanumān and Sugrīva. The latter was anointed king after his brother Vālī had been killed. Their capital was Pampā which lay in the region of Tuṅgabhadrā. Thus, the setting was in the present-day Karnataka region.

In this context it is important to note that the author of *Rāmachandracharita*, Nāgachandra, records a tradition that the ancient inhabitants of Kiṣkindhā were not monkeys but a tribe whose banner carried the insignia of a monkey.

Perhaps the earliest rendering of the life-story of Rāma in the Kannada language is in the *Chāvundarāya Purāṇa* ascribable to circa 978 CE. However, it deviates here and there from the *Rāmāyaṇa* of Vālmīki. We may refer to another noteworthy work in the Kannada language, namely *Rāmachandra-charita Purāṇa*, popularly known as the *Pampā Rāmāyaṇa*, by an eleventh-century poet named Nāgachandra. Written towards the end of the sixteenth century is the *Rāmakathā* of Narahari, which is by and large a rendering of the *Rāmāyaṇa* of Vālmīki. It is because of this that Narahari is also known as 'Kumāra Vālmīki '. That the Rāmāyaṇa theme has all along been very popular in Karnataka may be adjudged from the fact that a 19th century poet, Muddaṇa, wrote three works, namely *Adbhuta Rāmāyaṇa, Rāmāśvamedha* and *Rāmapaṭṭābhiṣeka*. In fact, even today ballads dealing with the life-story of Rāma are being composed and sung.

In terms of the portrayal of the life of Rāma in art, Karnataka has a lot to offer. However, we shall deal with it a little later.

6. In Tamil Nadu

Right at the beginning we had referred to the Kāśakuḍī plate inscription of Nandivarman, dated to 752-53 CE, in which the king's skill in archery has been compared with that of Rāma. This inscription also refers to one of the predecessors of

Nandivarman, namely Narasiṁhavarman, as having "surpassed the glory of the valour of Rāma by (his) conquest of Laṅkā". Indeed, references to the story of Rāma occur in the earliest part of the *Sangama* literature of Tamil Nadu, dating back to a period almost as old as the *Rāmāyaṇa* of Vālmīki. For example, a verse in the *Puranānūru* collection states that while being carried away by Rāvaṇa, after her abduction, Sītā consciously dropped her ornaments down so that these may lead to her being traced out. As would be discussed a little later, this very theme forms the subject-matter of a terracotta representation from Kauśāmbī, ascribable to the 2nd-1st century BCE (Fig. 1.10).

We may now refer to Kamban, the most celebrated poet of Tamil Nadu. While some scholars think that he lived in the 9th century CE, others put his period in the 12th century. Be that as it may, his *Rāmāyaṇa* is doubtless such a superb and engrossing piece of literature that even today it is held in great respect. "There must be something timeless", says the renowned author S. Maharajan (1972: 8) "about a poet who has gripped the attention of the people for over a millennium".

C. NON-BRĀHMAṆICAL SOURCES OF THE STORY OF RĀMA

The antiquity of the Rāmāyaṇa story is also verifiable from non-Brāhmaṇical sources, such as the Buddhist and Jain literature.

1. In Buddhist Literature

In the Buddhist literature there are the *Jātaka*s, three of which deal with the story of Rāma. The *Jātaka*s form a part of the *Khuddaka-nikāya*, ascribable to the 3rd century BCE. **The most noteworthy of these is the one called *Daśaratha Jātaka*. Herein, however, Rāma is referred to as Rāma-paṇḍita, Lakṣmaṇa as Lakṣmaṇa-kumāra and Bharata as Bharata-kumāra.** The *Jātaka* story differs in certain details from that in the *Rāmāyaṇa* of Vālmīki. As for example, the scene is set in

Vāraṇasī instead of Ayodhyā. However, as the *Jātaka* story goes, when Bharata-kumāra went to meet Rāma-panḍiṭa during the course of the latter's exile and communicated to him the news of their father's death, Rāma-panḍita remained extremely composed and said: "No amount of weeping can bring the dead back to life, so the wise do not lament over the death of any one...." Rāma-panḍita did not return but gave to Bharata-kumāra his sandals as his symbol and asked him to go back and rule the kingdom on the former's behalf. and so on.

The other two *Jātaka*s are the '*Nidāna* of the King of Ten Luxuries' and the '*Jātaka* of the Unnamed King'. Unfortunately, the originals are lost, but these are preserved in their Chinese translations. The former was translated by one Kekaya in 472 CE, while the latter by a Sogdian monk named Kan-Seng-hui in 251 CE. The carry-over of these *Jātaka* stories to China only serves to emphasize how popular was the Rāma story even with the Buddhists. The deviations in detail are easily explained by the immense time-lag between the actual happenings and their narration in the Buddhist texts.

2. In Jain Literature

The Jain *Rāmāyaṇa*s are not only in Sanskrit, but also in Prākṛita, Apabhraṁśa and even Kaṇṇaḍa. A canonical work, *Anuyogadvāra*, supposed to date back to the 2nd century CE, lists many other works which include the *Rāmāyaṇam*. However, for sure, *Pauma-chariyam* by Vimala Sūri, assignable to the 5th century CE, is the earliest rendering of the life-story of Rāma. The book, however, deviates sometimes from the *Rāmāyaṇa* of Vālmīki.

Another noteworthy Rāmāyaṇa text is *Vasudevahiṇḍī*, also assignable to the 5th century CE. The Rāma-kathā tradition continued on and on and here mention may be made of some of the works: the *Rāmāyaṇa* by Svayambhū in Apabhraṁśa (8th century CE); *Mahāpurāṇa* by Pushpadanta in Prākṛita (10th century); *Pampā Rāmāyaṇa* by Nāgachandra (11th century) and *Jina Rāmāyaṇa* by Chandrasāgara Varṇī (19th century).

The Jain tradition holds that the Vidyādharas were human beings, and were the descendants of Nami and Vinami, sons of Ṛiśabhadeva; and the **Vānaras were a section of the Vidyādharas, who adopted the insignia of the monkey.**

3. In Persian Literature

So much attracted was Akbar (1556-1605 CE) by the life-story of Rāma that he asked Quader Badauni to translate the *Rāmāyaṇa* in Persian, adding that the work be finished within four years; and the latter duly complied (see above, p. 6). Akbar's example was followed by his son and successor, Jahangir. During his reign, Sa'dulla' Masihi Panipati produced an excellent translation of the *Rāmāyaṇa* in Persian. And what is no less interesting is that in order to learn Sanskrit, Masihi Panipati spent twelve years in Banaras (now called Vārāṇasī). A couplet extols Sītā's purity in these words: "Even the garments did not see her naked body as the soul which is within the body is not seen by it."

Many Hindu poets too composed the *Rāmāyaṇa* in the Persian language. Amongst them, mention may be made of Amanat Rai Layalpuri and Girdhardas.

D. RĀMA'S STORY BEYOND THE FRONTIERS OF INDIA

The story of Rāma's life seems to have been so fascinating that it transcended the frontiers of the country and reached in the north to Mongolia, in the north-east to Japan, and in the south-east to as far as the Philippines. Sri Lanka, of course, was a part of the play itself. Here, however, we shall deal with only a few of these regions as samples, and that too rather briefly.

1. Sri Lanka

There are many sites in Sri Lanka associated with the Rāmāyaṇa story. However, in terms of literary texts, particular mention may be made of *Jānakī-haraṇa*, an excellent poetic composition by Kumāradāsa who lived in the 7th century CE. Besides, there exists a popular version as well which is in use even today.

2. Tibet

Documents containing the Tibetan version of the *Rāmāyaṇa* were discovered by Aurel Stein and Paul Pelliot and are now kept in the Bibliotheque Nationale in Paris and the India Office Library, London. These documents are ascribable to a time between 700 and 900 CE. The story contained in them has quite a few variation from that in the *Rāmāyaṇa* of Vālmīki. Thus, for example, Daśaratha is stated to have had only two wives, instead of three, and two sons in place of four. The names of the sons are given as Rāmana and Laksane (instead of Lakṣmaṇa).

3. China

Rāma's story found its way into China through Buddhism and occurs there in the form of two *Jātaka*s. It is interesting to note that while their Indian versions are missing, the Chinese ones are available. One of them, named *Anāmaka Jātaka* (known as the Jātaka of the Unnamed King) and was translated into Chinese in 251 CE by a Sogdian monk, Kan-seng-hui. The other one, known as '*Nidāna* of the King of ten Luxuries', was translated in 472 CE, most probably by Kekaya.

As might be expected, in the case of such transferences many deviations find their way. Thus, for example, in the 'Jātaka of the Unnamed King', Rāma is called a Bodhisattava. Further, the Bodhisattva left his kingdom with his wife and went to the forest because of 'a quarrel with his wicked uncle'. Again, instead of a Rākṣasa, it was a Nāga who came, posing as a sage, and abducted the wife of the Bodhisattva. And so on. Similar is the case with the other *Jātaka*. According to it, Daśaratha had four wives, instead of three in the *Rāmāyaṇa* of Vālmīki. However, much of the story is duly included: for instance, the banishment of Rāma, the death of Daśaratha, Bharata's persuasion of Rāma to return, the latter's refusal to do so and finally the return of Rāma after the full period of banishment.

4. JAPAN

The *Anāmaka Jātaka* found its way into Japan as well. It occurs in a Japanese work Hobutsushu, assignable to the 12th century CE.

5. THAILAND

Amongst the south-eastern countries, Thailand seems to have witnessed the maximum influence of the Rāmāyaṇa story. For example, one of its capitals was even named as Ayodhyā, wherefrom kings of various dynasties ruled from 1350 to 1767 CE. However, dated to a still earlier time (1292 CE) is an inscription of the reign of King Rāma Khamhaeng, which refers to the story of Rāma. (Also, please note the first part of the name of the king.) Shadow-plays even today keep the story of Rāma alive.

6. MALAYASIA

Even though largely populated by Muslims now, Malayasia has retained the Rāma tradition, both through literature as well as orally. The literary aspect is represented by *Hikayet Seri Rāma* (*Seri* being equivalent of Sanskrit *Śrī*). The puppet shows are accompanied by ballads sung with great gusto.

7. CAMBODIA

The famous temple of Ankor Vat, to which we shall refer in some detail a little later, contains several representations from Rāma's life. On the literary side, one may refer to *Rāma-kertī* (*kertī* being equivalent to Sanskrit *kīrtī*). While the date of its composition is not known, the available manuscript is ascribable to the 17th century CE.

8. Indonesia

This is yet another country dominated by Muslim population. Nevertheless, it too has retained the Rāma tradition. No visitor to Java can afford to miss the excellent performance of dance-dramas based on the Rāmāyaṇa story. On the literary side, one may refer to the *Rāmāyaṇa Kakawin*, which is the oldest version, based on the *Rāmāyaṇa* of Vālmīki. However, the earliest known evidence related to the Rāmāyaṇa story as such is in the form of an inscription (732 CE) of king Sanjaya whose *digvijaya* (conquest) is compared to that of Raghu, an ancestor of Rāma. Other inscriptions too, dated between 824 and 928 CE, refer to Sītā, Lakṣmaṇa, Rāvaṇa, etc. But what is most breath-taking is the superb portrayal of a number of scenes from the *Rāmāyaṇa* in the temples at Prāmbanam, dated to the 9th century CE.

9. Philippines

Is it not surprising that the life-story of Rāma reached as far east as Philippines? In this context mention may be made of *Maharadia Lawana* which is a brief version of the *Rāmāyaṇa*. The word *Maharadia* is equivalent to Sanskrit *Mahārāja*, while *Lawana* is Rāvaṇa. Interesting also is the fact that Rāvaṇa becomes an eminent personage in the Philippine version.

A Thought

Wondering at the above-mentioned immense spread of the life-story of Rāma – over thousands of years and thousands of kilometres – and pondering over the initial question we set out to answer, viz. 'Was Rāma a real-life person or mythical?', one is reminded of the old saying: "You can bluff some people for some time, some others for all time, but not all for all time".

E. EVIDENCE OF A PURELY SECULAR TEXT

While it is normal for religious texts to deal with the life-story of Rāma, it is interesting to find that even non-religious, purely secular, ancient texts indirectly refer to him. In this context, a reference may here be made to the *Arthaśāstra*, the well known treatise by Kauṭilya. It deals with administrative and allied matters and has nothing to do with any religion. Kauṭilya is reputed to have been instrumental in the overthrowing of the last king of the Nanda Dynasty and the anointment of Chandragupta Maurya as the king. Thus, his above-mentioned work may safely be placed towards the end of the 4th century BCE. It would then follow that the *Arthaśāstra* is a trifle earlier than even the *Rāmāyaṇa* of Vālmīki.

The *Arthaśāstra* comprises fifteen *Adhikaraṇa*s (Books); and each *Adhikaraṇa* has a number of *Adhyāya*s (Chapters). The first *Adhikaraṇa* is captioned as *Vinayādhikārika* and deals with 'Discipline'. Its sixth *Adhyāya* is titled as *Indriya-jaya*, i.e. 'Restraint of the Organs of Sense', with a sub-title 'The Shaking off of the Aggregate of the Six Enemies'. In it Kauṭilya recommends the abandoning of the following six enemies, namely *kāma* (lust), *krodha* (anger), *lobha* (greed), *māna* (vanity), *mada* (haughtiness) and *harṣa* (overjoy). He then proceeds to give examples how various kings and big personalities of the past suffered adversely on account of having succumbed to these. He begins by citing the example of "Bhoja, known also by the name of Dāṇḍakya, who, making a lascivious attempt on a Brāhmaṇa maiden, perished along with his kingdom and relations".

Proceeding further on, he states as follows:

mānādrāvaṇaḥ paradārānaprayachchhan.
Duryodhano rājyādaṁśam cha,

which, translated into English would be:

Rāvaṇa, unwilling under the influence of vanity to restore a stranger's wife, as well as Duryodhana to part with a portion of his kingdom.

These two perished, according to Kauṭilya, respectively because the former abducted the wife of a stranger and the latter refused to part with even a portion of his kingdom. The reference in the second anecdote is evidently to the story of the *Mahābhārata*. Then what about the first one? Does it not refer to the *Rāmāyaṇa* ? Verily, it does. **The wife of a 'stranger' 'not restored by Rāvaṇa' is definitely none other than Sītā. Taking the logic further, if, according to Kauṭilya, Rāvaṇa was a historical figure, the historicity of Rāma gets established *ipso facto*. Any doubts?**

F. ARCHAEOLOGY COMES INTO THE PICTURE

1. Introductory

When the Britishers left India in 1947, there was an yawning gap in our knowledge of ancient Indian history. We had at the one end of the scale the Harappan Civilization which, in its Mature Stage, ranged in date from circa 2600 to 2000 BCE and on the other the period of the *Ṣoḍaśa Mahājanapada*s (Sixteen Big States) beginning around the sixth century BCE. Archaeologically, very little was known about the intermediary period and thus it was loosely termed as the 'Dark Age', although there was nothing 'dark' about it. It was indeed a great challenge for Indian archaeologists.

As Superintending Archaeologist in charge of the Excavations Branch of the Archaeological Survey of India, I was privileged to be a part of these investigations. Straightaway, I began exploring some ancient sites in western Uttar Pradesh, which had so far received scanty attention. At many of these sites I found a distinctive pottery, grey in colour and painted in black pigment with a variety of geometric, linear and curvilinear designs. It was given a proper name, the Painted Grey Ware (PGW). In the naturally exposed vertical sections of the mounds concerned it was also observed that this ware lay in almost the lowest levels, much below the material known to belong to the 6th-5th centuries BCE. In 1950

I published a paper captioned 'The Painted Grey Ware of the Upper Gangetic Basin: An Approach to the Problems of the Dark Age'.

Since many of the sites that yielded this particular pottery were associated with the Mahābhārata story, I decided to undertake excavation at Hastināpura, which was the capital of the Kauravas. Over here is a large mound, located on the right bank of the Gaṅgā in Meerut District of Uttar Pradesh. Without going into the details, it is relevant to state that the excavations revealed that a sizeable portion of the Painted Grey Ware settlement was washed away by a heavy flood in the Gaṅgā (Fig. 1.2). Further, a part of the washed-away material, including a few sherds of the PGW were also encountered in the nearly 15-metre-deep bore-holes in the adjacent bed of the river (Fig. 1.3; also see Lal 1954-55). A comparison of this archaeological evidence with that from literature was highly telling. The relevant part of the text runs as follows:

Gaṅgayāpahṛite tasmin nagare Nāgasāhvaye
Tyaktvā Nichakṣur nagaram Kauśāmbyām sa nivatsyati

After the washing away of the site of Hastināpura by the Gaṅgā, (the then ruler) Nichakṣu will abandon it and move (the capital) to Kauśāmbī.

Archaeologically, what is no less exciting is that the lowest levels of Kauśāmbī began with the same kind of material culture as was there in existence at Hastināpura at the time when the flood destroyed it.

The texts further mention the names of the rulers of Kauśāmbī, according to which Udayana was twenty-fifth from Nichakṣu. It is well known that Udayana was a contemporary of Buddha, whose commonly accepted date is 565- 487 BCE. In other words, Udayana may have been ruling around 500 BCE. Though the average reign per ruler has been a matter of debate, an estimate worked out on the basis of known dynasties of ancient and mediaeval India places the average around 14 years. Thus the approximate date of Nichakṣu would be

Fig. 1.2. Hastināpura: A heavy flood in the Gaṅgā cut away a major portion of the Painted Grey Ware settlement at the site. The man points out the erosion-line.

Fig. 1.3. Hastināpura: A part of the washed-away material was discovered in the bores in the river-bed, some 15 metres below the water-level.

around 850 BCE. Further, since, according to the same texts, Nichakṣu was the 5th ruler of Hastināpura, after the Mahābhārata war, the war may broadly be placed around the 10th century BCE. **Anyway, the important point is that literary and archaeological evidences have both converged to establish the historicity of the *Mahābhārata*, though clearly it is nobody's claim that each and every detail mentioned therein is archaeologically verifiable. Further, let it not be forgotten that the *Mahābhārata* is a *prabandha-kāvya* (an epic) in the writing of which the poet enjoyed full freedom of imagination.**

The readers will kindly forgive me for this seemingly unwanted and long introduction. But I thought it was necessary to let the readers know how, encouraged by the results (though by no means immense) of my excavation at Hastināpura, I embarked upon my next project, namely 'Archaeology of the Rāmāyaṇa Sites'. Though conceived while in the Survey, I could not undertake it since as the Director General almost all my time was taken up by administrative and other allied matters. It was only after my voluntary retirement from the Survey in 1972 that I could plan to take up this project, to begin with at the Jiwaji University, Gwalior, and later with full attention at the Indian Institute of Advanced Study at Shimla. The Survey helped me in the field-work which ran from 1977 to 1986, by deputing the staff of its Excavations Branch, which for most of the time was headed by Shri K.N. Dikshit.

Under this project, five sites were taken up for investigation: (i) Ayodhyā, the capital of the Kosala kingdom, from where Rāma hailed; (ii) Śṛiṅgaverapura, where Rāma, Sītā and Lakṣmaṇa crossed the Gaṅgā in the first lap of their exile; (iii) Bharadvāja Āśrama, where the trio stayed overnight to pay their homage to sage Bharadvāja; (iv) Chitrakūṭa, where they stayed for quite some time before proceeding southwards; and (v) Nandigrāma from where Bharata carried on the governmental affairs in the absence of Rāma (cf. the map,

Fig. 1.4). This being not the forum for a detailed report on these excavations, we will confine ourselves to a very brief summary of the findings.[1]

2. Ayodhyā

Located on the right bank of the Sarayū, in District Faizabad, Uttar Pradesh, Ayodhyā was the capital of the Kosala kingdom in ancient times. The mound over here is fairly large, covering an area of about a square kilometre and rising at places to a height of 10 metres. Excavations were carried out at fourteen spots, located in different parts of the site, in order to ensure that the lowest levels were not missed in case these existed in some areas and not in others. These included certain well known localities like the Janma-Bhūmi (Fig. 1.5), Hanumān-garhī, Kauśilyā Ghāṭa, Nala-Tīlā, etc.

The excavations revealed that the settlement at Ayodhyā began with a phase when a very distinctive and deluxe pottery called the Northern Black Polished Ware (NBPW) had come into being. It is a highly shining ware with surface-colour varying from jet black, indigo, silvery to golden. The shapes too are the ones that dominate in the early stage of the ware, such as convex-sided dishes and bowls with corrugated profile.

Tools of iron, besides those of copper, also characterized the NBPW levels. These could be used for domestic chores, agriculture and even for warfare. In due course of time, weights of fine-grained stones made their appearance, as did a system of coinage. The NBPW-period weights are cylindrical, in marked contrast to those of the Harappan Civilization,

1. In 1991 I submitted a comprehensive Report on the unique tank discovered at Śṛiṅgaverapura (see below), which was published in 1993. Since then I have written more than a dozen letters to the Director General, Archaeological Survey of India, to provide the necessary facilities for writing out reports on the other sites, but without any positive response. I am still hoping against hope!

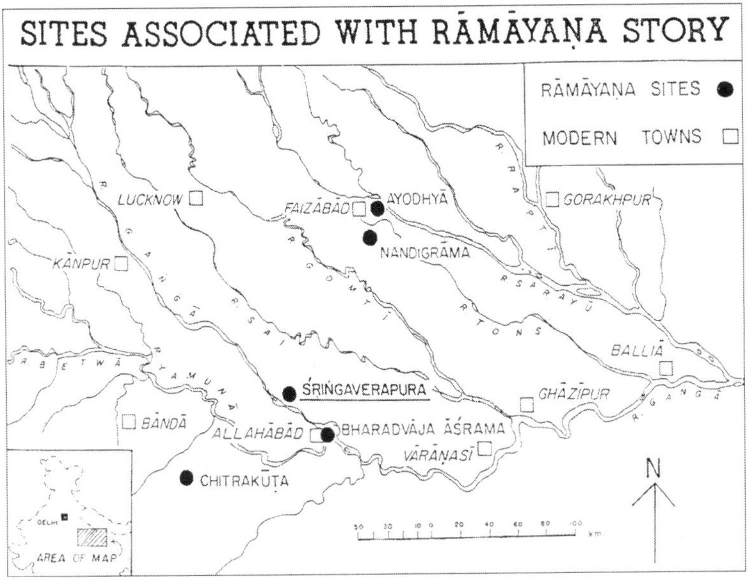

Fig. 1.4. Sites associated with the Rāmāyaṇa story.

which are cubical. The coins were the earliest to be produced in the country. These were made of silver or copper and bore on their surface punched marks. There were no inscriptions on them mentioning the names of the rulers, as became the practice later on. (In this context, it may perhaps be worth while to mention that the Harappans did not have any coinage, and must have managed their trade-transactions through some other means.) To begin with, the structures were of mud or mud bricks, but as time passed kiln-fired bricks also came to be used. Way up in the NBPW period itself writing also emerged.

Without any break, the settlement continued through what are known as the Śuṅga, Kushan and Gupta periods. Since in the present context we are not much concerned with these periods, we skip their details. However, it may be well worth making a reference to an inscription discovered some time ago, though not at Ayodhyā itself, but in its suburb called Ranopali. Engraved on a stone slab and datable to the first

Fig. 1.5. Ayodhyā: View of one of the excavated trenches in the Janma-Bhūmi area.

century BCE, the inscription refers to the construction of a *ketana* (shrine?) by Dhanadeva, who has been mentioned as *Kosalādhīpa* i.e. 'king of Kosala'. He was sixth from Puṣyamitra who, according to the inscription, was an army general (*senāpati*) and had performed two horse-sacrifices (*dviraśvamedhayājinaḥ*). This Puṣyamitra was evidently the same who killed the last Mauryan ruler Bṛihadratha, and usurped the throne. What is important for us in the present context is that Ayodhyā continued to be the capital of the Kosala kingdom even up to the beginning of the Common Era.

Whereas some parts of Ayodhyā were deserted after the Gupta period, Hanumān-garhī and Janma-Bhūmi areas were re-occupied around the 11-12th centuries CE. In the latter area, the uppermost levels of a trench that lay immediately to the south of the Babari Masjid, a series of brick-cum-stone bases were discovered (Fig. 2.1), over which there evidently once stood stone pillars. In this context it may be mentioned that affixed to the piers of the Masjid there were stone pillars bearing Hindu motifs and sculptures (to which a detailed reference will be made in the next chapter).

3. ŚṚIṄGAVERAPURA

It comprises a massive mound on the left bank of the Gaṅgā, in District Allahabad of Uttar Pradesh. Since the river takes a curve hugging the mound it has cut away a sizeable portion of the latter. Nevertheless, there still remains quite a lot to give a good picture of the various occupational strata at the site.

Unlike Ayodhyā, Śṛiṅgaverapura had an earlier beginning. In the lowest levels there occurred what is known in archaeological parlance as the 'Ochre Colour Ware' (OCP). It is a red ware, sometimes slipped and even bearing painted designs in black pigment. At certain sites this ware has been found in association with harpoons, antennae swords, anthropomorphic figures, etc. which have been termed as "Copper Hoards'. Broadly speaking, this cultural complex is datable from circa 2000 BCE to about the middle of the second millennium BCE. At Śṛiṅgaverapura, however, the OCP-occupation seems to have been short-lived, the potsherds too occurring in a very sporadic manner. From this period to the next there is a break of occupation. The latter is characterized in the lowest levels by Black-slipped and Black-and-red wares, immediately followed by the well known Northern Black Polished Ware. The deposits of this latter period yielded the same kind of material culture as did the corresponding strata of Ayodhyā. These were followed by occupations associated successively with the Śuṅga, Kushan and Gupta times. After a break, the site was re-occupied in the 12th century CE, as indicated by the presence of a large number of coins of the Gahaḍavāla ruler, Govinda Chandra. Thereafter the site was also inhabited during the Late Mediaeval and even in the East India Company times; with the details of these periods, however, we are not concerned at least in the present context.

However, it may well be worth while to let the readers know about a very noteworthy discovery made at this site, even though it has no bearing whatsoever on the subject-matter of this booklet. It relates to a unique system of water-supply arrangement made around the beginning of the Common Era. By this time the population of the site had considerably increased and thus a need was felt to keep the supply of water ready at hand for the residents who lived away from the river-bank. To the north of the mound there is a *nullah* which drains the rain-water from the higher areas into the river. However, during heavy floods in the Gaṅgā, the water-level is so high that the flood-water goes upstream in the *nullah* for a considerable distance. Noticing this phenomenon year after year, the local engineers decided to harness the flood water and store it in a 250-metre long tank-complex. Thus, they cut a channel into this *nullah* and, through it, diverted the flood-water to an area where they had planned to construct the reservoir. Without going into the details, it may briefly be stated that this tank-complex had all the constituents that a modern engineer would ask for, namely a silting chamber, a silting tank, the main tank, a ritual tank and finally the waste-weir, from where, by means of an exit channel, the excess water was sent back to the Gaṅgā.

Rough calculations show that the storage capacity of the tank-complex was about 7.5 billion litres, which normally would have sufficed for the period from September to June, after which, in July, fresh supply was available. But the Śṛiṅgaverapura engineers were not content with this. Thus, to meet any short-fall of water-supply, they took recourse to a supplementary device. They dug a series of wells (Fig. 1.6) in the bed of the main tank, carrying these down to the sub-soil water. Thus, even in an emergency water-supply was duly assured.

4. Bharadvāja Āśrama

In Allahabad, Uttar Pradesh, there is a locality known as Bharadvāja Āśrama, diagonally opposite Anand Bhavan, the ancestral house of the Nehru family. It is flat piece of land without any sign of a mound, such as we have at Ayodhyā and Śṛiṅgaverapura. The local Municipality has laid a park

Fig. 1.6. Śṛiṅgaverapura: View of a part of the tank ascribable to the beginning of the Common Era. In the bed may be seen one of the wells going down to the sub-soil water-level.

Fig. 1.7. Bharadvāja Āśrama: There is no mound at the site. It is a flat piece of land, in level with the surrounding ground.

over it and the only indication of its ever having been associated with sage Bharadvāja is a late mediaeval temple dedicated to him. The total absence of a mound was very puzzling. However, I argued within myself that if there was any truth in the association of the site with sage Bharadvāja it must yield the ancient remains.

With this kind of apprehensive inquisitiveness, I started excavating the flat piece of land (Fig. 1.7). One long and a couple of small trenches were put up to ensure a thorough combing. And lo and behold, hardly within 25-30 centimetres from the surface, we struck structures of kiln-fired bricks. Two such structural levels were met with, one below the other (Fig. 1.8). There were a lot of associated pottery, terracotta figurines, inscribed seals – all of which belonged to the Gupta period, viz. fourth-fifth centuries CE. But when we dug deeper we did not come across any structures. But what we did meet was no less telling. There was a 2-3-metre thick deposit of sandy loam in which there occurred sporadically potsherds

Fig. 1.8. Bharadvāja Āśrama: A view of another trench. In it two successive structures were met with in the upper levels. Lower down there were deposits of sandy loam which yielded sporadically sherds of the Northern Black Polished Ware as well as lumps of clay with reed-marks, indicating wattle-and-daub huts in an *āśrama*-like setting.

of the Northern Black Polished and Black-slipped wares. There were no regular occupational floors. At the same time, lumps of clay bearing impression of reeds were met with (Fig. 1.9). Altogether, the picture was that of a sporadic occupation with some wattle-and-daub huts.

5. Chitrakūṭa

At present the town of Chitrakūṭa falls partly in Uttar Pradesh and partly in Madhya Pradesh. The adjacent river is Mandākinī, on both the banks of which the ancient settlement is located. However, the mounds are overridden by so many mediaeval and modern temples that it was next to impossible to get enough space for any worthwhile excavation. Thus, we had to be content with only section-scrappings. From these, however, sherds of Black-slipped and NBP wares were picked up, throwing light on the antiquity of the site.

6. Nandīgrāma

During the period of Rāma's exile, Bharata is said to have carried on the administrative functions not from Ayodhyā but from a place called Nandīgrāma. However, he did not live in that town but seems to have chosen to live in somewhat lonely place now identified as Bharata-Kuṇḍa. There is no mound over here but not far away there does exist a mound which may represent the ancient site. A small-scale excavation over here brought to light in the lowest levels the same culture-complex as did Ayodhyā and hence the details are not repeated here.

7. A Brief Analysis of the Results from the Excavated Sites

The evidence from the excavations at the foregoing five sites shows that the earliest time when all these were under occupation was that of the Northern Black Polished Ware (NBPW). The only exception is that of Śṛiṅgaverapura where a still earlier occupation is indicated by the presence of the

Fig. 1.9. Bharadvāja Āśrama: A lump of clay with reed-marks, suggesting the presence of wattle-and-daub huts.

Ochre Colour Ware. Anyway, it is the NBPW that ties these sites together. The next relevant question is: how early do these NBPW strata go in terms of absolute time? The scientific technique that helps in determining this is known as the Carbon-14 method. Very simply put, the charcoal obtained from a given stratum is tested by this technique, which gives the time that has elapsed since the wood concerned was burnt, turning into charcoal. There, of course, is a small margin of error in the determination and the same is also recorded. The date thus obtained is further calibrated and the final result gives us an approximate idea of the time when the wood got converted into charcoal. With the date of the charcoal thus obtained, it is possible to fix the date of the occupation-deposits from which the charcoal had been collected.

Charcoal samples collected by the present writer, which were from the upper NBPW levels at Ayodhyā, gave a date-range from the 6th to 3rd centuries BCE. But the lower levels remained to be properly dated. This very important lacuna has since been filled up by putting to test the charcoal samples collected from the lower NBPW levels by the Archaeological Survey during its renewed excavations (2002-03) in the Janma-Bhūmi area (short-named AYD-1). The dating was done by the laboratory of the Birbal Sahni Institute of Palaeobotany, Lucknow. The relevant details of their findings, as quoted by S. C. Saran (Saran 2006:25), are as follows:

Field-sample No., Layer No. and depth in metres	B.S. lab. No.	Age of sample, based on half-life 5570 ± 30 yrs.	Calibrated Range in BCE
No. 1A, AYD-1	2126	2730 ± 80 BP (780 BCE)	970-810 BCE
No. 7, AYD-1, G-7, Layer 16, 9.15m	2152	2830 ± 100 BP (880 BCE)	1190-840 BCE
No. 8, AYD-1, G-7, Layer 19, 11m	2153	2860 ± 100 BP (910 BCE)	1210-900 BCE
No. 9, AYD-1, G-7 Layer 20, 11.53m	2154	3200 ± 130 BP (1250 BCE)	1980-1320 BCE

I do not know if the sample bearing BS No.2154 comes from the lowest level. In any case, the above-mentioned C-14 dates indicate that the lower levels of the NBPW do go back to a period well before 1000 BCE.

While no doubt the excavations at the above-mentioned five sites do establish that all these were characterized by the same kind of cultural equipment in their lower levels and were in existence around the beginning of the first millennium BCE, the excavations have not thrown up any inscriptional evidence to show that the sites were associated with the Rāmāyaṇa story as such. In this context, however, the evidence yielded by Bharadvāja Āśrama is of utmost significance, as would be seen from the following discussion.

Let it be assumed, for the sake of argument, that the Rāmāyaṇa story was the figment of imagination of a poet called Vālmīki. It is accepted by scholars that the *Rāmāyaṇa* of Vālmīki was reduced to writing some time between the third century

BCE and third century CE. During this time-bracket, whereas the other sites associated with the Rāmāyaṇa story were 'living entities' (i.e. under occupation), as demonstrated by the excavations, that of Bharadvāja Āśrama was not. A question that now needs to be asked is: How come that this last-named site was also included in the narrative of Vālmīki when it was not a 'living entity'? One may well weave a story and include in it the names of sites that exist at that point of time or are known to have existed once, but not of places that never existed. Thus, the only possible way in which the inclusion of Bharadvāja Āśrama in the Vālmīki *Rāmāyaṇa* can be explained is that there must have already existed, perhaps in the form of a ballad, a core story in which this site also featured and it was this prevalent story that was reduced to writing in the third-second century BCE.

In this context, there are three very significant pieces of evidence from Bharadvāja Āśrama which call for a proper interpretation. First of all, it is the topography of the site. As already stated, it consists of a flat piece of land there being no evidence of any mound, the like of which we have at Ayodhyā or Śṛiṅgaverapura. But right adjacent to it the ground-level drops by 5-6 metres and the slope continues as one moves on towards the Gaṅgā. Local people tell us that not long ago the flood-waters of the Gaṅgā, when it was in spate during the rainy season, used to come up far inside. A bund that has since been constructed prevents the water from coming up now. In other words, all this indicates that in ancient times the Gaṅgā used to flow past the Bharadvāja Āśrama.

Secondly, as already mentioned earlier, the lower levels of Bharadvāja Āśrama did not yield any brick structures as did the upper levels. Nevertheless, sherds of the Northern Black Polished Ware did occur, but only sporadically, in the thick sandy loam that lay under the brick structures. Also met with were lumps of clay bearing impressions of reed, which indicated that there were only wattle-and-daub huts in the area. This scenario fits well into the picture of an *āśrama* (hermitage) by the side of the Gaṅgā. Surely, Archaeology cannot tell us that it was the Aśrama of Bharadvāja, since we have not come across any inscription from the site certifying the same. For all we know, writing was not in vogue at that time. The earliest inscription that we have are datable to the third century BCE.

The third point of interest is that, as already mentioned, the site was re-occupied only during the Gupta times. It is well known that it was during the Gupta period that there took place a great revival of the Brāhmaṇical religion. Since oral tradition, perhaps through ballads, must have carried down the centuries the memory of the association of this site with the Rāma story, it was but natural for the people to revive its glory by re-occupying it.

In the above context, it may also not be out of place to state that even today ballads based on certain noteworthy contemporary events are being composed and sung, though print and electronic media are in full operation. And I give here an example. It was a cold winter morning in 1954. I was travelling by the Kalka Mail from Calcutta (now re-named Kolkata) to New Delhi. As the train halted at Allahabad, I saw thousands of people running up and down the various platforms. They were desperately seeking to get into the trains, some stationed and others steaming in. As I opened the door of my compartment to look out at what was going on, about fifty people got into it forcing me to find a shelter at the far end of my berth. Some of the people were in tears, some others were shouting and cursing the local authorities. I just couldn't make out the head and tail of it all. As the train steamed out the commotion lessened and in due course of time these passengers alighted at their respective stations. Late in the evening I reached my home and after a quiet dinner went to sleep. Next morning when the newspaper arrived, I saw on the front page a banner-heading stating how a major calamity had befallen the people in Allahabad, who had assembled there to participate in the *Kumbha Melā*. (This is a very important festival in which pilgrims come from far and wide to have a dip in the holy Gaṅgā.) The newspaper gave a long narrative of the event. Briefly, however, when the mass of humanity had gathered for the dip, a procession of *Nāgā*

Sādhūs (naked mendicants), some on foot and others seated on decorated elephants, suddenly appeared on the scene. For some unexplained reason the elephants ran amok and overran some of the pilgrims. In the utter confusion that followed hundreds of people lost their lives. The civil authorities did whatever they could under the very taxing circumstances, though a tragedy of immeasurable magnitude had already taken place.

Now, while the newspapers and electronic media duly reported the event and the subsequent judicial enquiry and steps taken by the government to compensate the people for their losses, the important point that this writer would like to bring to the notice of the readers is that this tragic event was, within a period of a few months, rendered in the form of ballads, of which three different versions are now in existence. Ballad-composers from Jhusi and Daryaganj, places right in Allahabad, and those from Śṛiṅgaverapura produced their own versions which, though different from one another in details, narrate the basics of the event. I had the occasion to listen to and tape-record the Śṛiṅgaverapura version which was sung to us one evening by one of the local workers at our excavation-camp (Lal 2002: 402-08). The actual recorded text is given the Appendix I. Here I give only the gist of it.

After offering obeisance to Sarasvatī, the Goddess of Learning, the composer praises the sacred river Gaṅgā and then gives a brief description of the locality he hails from. Thereafter he gives the details of the incident. Says he (a summary rendering of which is as follows):

> It was the year 1954. There was a public announcement that the *melā* (festival gathering) was going to be a big affair. All sorts of administrative arrangements were made such as deputing the police, starting new trains for the *melā* and even constructing an air-strip. When the 3rd of February arrived – it was a Wednesday – people came in large numbers for taking their bath. From one end the pilgrims pushed their way and from the opposite direction *Sādhūs* did the same. There was a terrible confusion near the *bund*. As a result, lots of people died: men, women, the old and young. The blind, lame and beggars – none was spared. They all made their way to *yama-*

> *loka* (the land of Death). So many members of various families died within the twinkling of the eye. Military lorries soon arrived at the scene, picked up the dead and injured and took them to the police station. Photographs were taken of the dead bodies, injured were taken to hospitals and announcements were made regarding the missing ones. And so on. At the end the composer of the ballad gives his name as Ram Adhar.

This description tallies, by and large, with what had appeared in the print and electronic media.

While camping at Śṛiṅgaverapura in connection with the excavations, I tape-recorded another *virahā* (ballad). It narrates the story of a gruesome murder of a person by his own sister for the sake of money. The brother, who had earned a lot of money by working in a far-away town and was carrying it on his person, halted the night at the sister's place on his way back to his native village. The sister, on learning that he had a lot of money with him, was tempted to get it by murdering him. She did commit the murder but was finally arrested. The case went to a court in Pratapgarh where the judge sentenced her to death. The entire story is verifiable from the records in the court.

The point that emerges from the above narratives is that even in the present century when the print and electronic media are in full operation some people choose to record certain noteworthy events through ballads. If this is the state of affairs even today, what would have prevented the local genius of the time from composing ballads about the thrilling story of Rāma, which evidently must have drawn the attention of one and all. As time moved and the ballad was passed on from generation to generation by word of mouth, and it was but natural for each new singer to add some *mirch-masālā* (spicy stuff) of his own. And when writing came to be used in the 3rd century BCE, the ballad assumed the form the epic known as the *Rāmāyaṇa* of Vālmīki.

G. PORTRAYAL OF RĀMA'S LIFE IN ART

Rāma's life has been depicted through a variety of art-media, such as terracottas, stone sculptures, bronzes and paintings.

Put together, these cover a very wide range of time, i.e. from the second century BCE right up to the present, and an equally long range of space, namely from India to Indonesia. Here, however, we can do no better than to present a few samples thereof.

1. In Terracotta

The earliest terracotta representation of a Rāmāyaṇic scene is that from Kauśāmbī in Uttar Pradesh. **Though not inscribed, on stylistic grounds it is ascribable to the 2nd-1st century BCE (Fig. 1.10). It depicts Rāvaṇa carrying Sītā away, after having abducted her.** A ferocious-looking Rāvaṇa is holding Sītā in his hands, and greatly worried, the latter is throwing away her ornaments on the ground, in the hope that some one might come across them and thereby be able to trace her whereabouts and communicate the same to Rāma. **This very scene is described in the *Rāmāyaṇa* of Vālmīki** (*Araṇya Kāṇḍa*, 54th *Sarga*, *Śloka*s 2 and 3) as follows:

> *Teṣām madhye viśālākṣī kauśeyam kanakaprbham /*
> *Uttarīyam varārohā śubhānyābharaṇāni cha /2/*
> *Mumocha yadi Rāmāya śaṁseyuriti bhāminī /*
> *Vastramutsṛijya tanmadhye nikṣiptam sahabhūṣaṇam /3/*

We then pass on to a **terracotta representation of Rāma himself (Fig. 1.11)**. At present it is lodged in the Los Angeles County Museum, USA, but is said to have come from Nachāra Kherā in Haryana. It has been executed in what is known as the Kushan style of art. The right hand is in the *abhaya-mudrā*. Behind the back on this very side may also be seen the upper part of the quiver filled with arrows. **However, what is most important is that the figure bears an inscription. It is located on the lower part of the garment. Written in the Brāhmī script of circa 3rd century CE, it reads *Rāma*, thereby not leaving any doubt about its identification.**

Fig. 1.10. Kauśāmbī: A 2nd-1st century BCE terracotta. It shows Rāvaṇa carrying away Sītā, after abducting her. She drops down her ornaments in the hope that these might be picked up by someone, which would help in tracing her whereabouts. This depiction tallies very well with the description in the *Rāmāyaṇa* of Vālmīki.

Fig. 1.11. A terracotta figure currently lodged in the Los Angeles County Museum of Art, USA, but believed to have come from Nachāra Kherā in Haryana. It portrays Rāma whose name is also inscribed, in Brāhmī characters of the 3rd century CE.

We now take up three more terracottas from Haryana. One of these, again from Nachāra Kherā, is shown on Fig. 1.12. Though its left part is broken, it is important because of the inscription it carries at the top. The available part of the inscription reads:

...... *chhan antarā raghunandanaḥ/ āsasāda mahāgṛidhaiḥ,*

which immediately reminds us of what is stated in the *Rāmāyaṇa* of Vālmīki (*Araṇya Kāṇḍa*, 14.1):

Atha Pañchvaṭīm gachchhannantarā raghunandanaḥ/
sasāda mahākāyam gṛidham bhīmaparākramam//

The context is that while going to Pañchavaṭī, Rāma met a strong vulture (Jaṭāyu) who gave certain clues about Sītā who had been abducted. This is precisely what the inscription on

Fig. 1.12. Nachāra Kherā, Haryana: An inscribed terracotta plaque depicting a scene from the *Rāmāyaṇa*. 4th century CE.

the terracotta plaque seeks to convey, though a good part of it is damaged. In the available part we see only Sītā with Lakṣmaṇa on her left. It is surmised that the broken part of the panel carried the figures of Rāma and Jaṭāyu. The delineation of the figures of both Sītā and Lakṣmaṇa is indeed superb. The script of the inscription is assignable to circa 4th century CE.

According to a plan hatched by Rāvaṇa, Mārīchi assumed the form of a golden deer and appeared before the cottage at Pañchavaṭī where Rāma, Sītā and Lakṣmaṇa were staying. On seeing the deer, Sītā asked Rāma to get the same for her. Rāma set out for the hunt and, as the story goes, there was a cry that Rāma was in trouble and needed urgent help. Lakṣmaṇa too left the cottage and Rāvaṇa, disguised as an ascetic, appeared on the scene and abducted Sītā. The terracotta panel, though damaged on the left (Fig. 1.13) clearly shows Rāma,

Fig. 1.13. Another terracotta panel from Nachāra Kherā, ascribable to the 4th century CE, depicting a scene from the *Rāmāyaṇa*.

Fig. 1.14. A terracotta panel from Jind, Haryana. It bears an inscription in Brāhmī characters of the 4th century CE, which refers to Hanumān as the destroyer of Aśoka Vāṭikā, in Laṅkā.

Sītā and the deer. The last-named is excellently depicted so as to show that it is running away. (The figure of Lakṣmaṇa is, however damaged.) On stylistic ground, this panel is similar to the one discussed earlier (Fig. 1.12) and is thus ascribable to circa 4th century CE. It too comes from Nachāra Kherā.

Coming from another site in Haryana, namely Jind, is a terracotta panel which depicts the destruction of a part of the Aśoka Vāṭikā by Hanumān, after having met Sītā. Though somewhat defaced, the panel clearly shows the destruction of the Aśoka Vāṭikā by Hanumān. As if to offset any doubts, the panel also bears an inscription, at the bottom (Fig. 1.14). It reads:

Hanumān Aśokavāṭikā hantā

in the Brāhmī script of circa 4th century CE.

2. In Stone

There are many temples all over the country which carry friezes relating to the life of Rāma. In point time too, these have a very wide range, from the 3rd century CE up to the modern times. Here, however, we remain content with giving just a couple of illustrations.

Down south, at Nāgārjunakoṇḍā in Andhra Pradesh, there is a very fine portrayal of the meeting of Bharata with Rāma at Chitrakūṭa (Fig. 1.15). It shows Rāma seated, while Bharata, standing in front of the former, entreats him to return to Ayodhyā. Behind Bharata is his entourage. It belongs to what is known as the Ikṣvāku School and is assignable to the 3rd century CE. What is no less important is that this depiction constitutes a part of the *Daśaratha Jātaka*, emphasizing once again that Rāma's life-story is not confined to Brāhmaṇical religion but also attracted the attention of the Buddhists.

From Chitrakūṭa, Rāma, Sītā and Lakṣmaṇa proceeded to Pañchavaṭī. It was here that the abduction of Sītā took place. A scene in a 5th century temple at Nāchanā-Kuṭhārā in Madhya

Fig. 1.15. Nāgārjunakoṇḍā, Andhra Pradesh. A stone panel depicting Bharata's meeting with Rāma at Chitrakūṭa, 3rd century CE.

Pradesh shows Rāvaṇa, in the guise of an ascetic, standing in front of the cottage of Sītā (Fig. 1.16). He requested her to give alms and when she came out to give him the alms he whisked her away.

Fig. 1.16. Nāchanā-Kuṭhārā, Madhya Pradesh: A stone panel depicting Rāvaṇa, guised as an ascetic, at Sītā's cottage in Pañchavaṭī. 5th century CE.

Fig. 1.17. Pāpanātha temple, Paṭṭadakala, Karnataka: The scene depicts the construction of a bridge over a part of the sea. 7th-8th century CE.

Rāma and Lakṣmaṇa then set out in search of Sītā. On their way, they met Hanumān and Sugrīva who helped them in their mission. It was learnt that Rāvaṇa, king of Laṅkā, had abducted her. Thus, an attack on Laṅkā became necessary, for which the part of sea between the tips of India and Laṅkā had to be bridged. A scene portrayed in the Pāpanātha Temple at Paṭṭadakala, Karnataka (Fig. 1.17) shows very graphically the Vānaras carrying stones on their heads and dumping the same in the sea. The sea is represented with wavy lines and in it are also seen the fishes. On the surface of the water lie rows of stones. The pillars and a lintel carry inscriptions in characters of the 7th-8th century CE.

3. In Paintings

Painting was yet another medium in which the life-story of Rāma was depicted. Most of these are ascribable to the mediaeval times. Here we first present a vivid painting in Malwa style, datable to the 17th century CE (Fig. 1.18). It depicts

Fig. 1.18. A 17th-century Malwa style painting. It depicts the boatman (*kevaṭa*) praying to Rāma to let the former wash the latter's feet, before letting Rāma get into the boat.

Fig. 1.19. A painting dated circa 1610 CE depicts the *agni-parīkṣā* (fire-ordeal) of Sītā.

the scene of Rāma's crossing the Gaṅgā at Śṛiṅgaverapura. As the texts say, the *kevaṭa* (boatman) did not agree to Rāma's getting into the boat without letting the former wash the feet of the latter. His (the boatman's) argument was that because, on an earlier occasion, the dust from Rāma's feet falling on a stone slab had turned it into a human being (namely Ahalyā), he was afraid that the same might happen to his boat, by which he would be deprived of it and thereby lose earning his bread. The picture shows the boatman beseeching Rāma with folded hands.

The other painting presented here is rather a rare one. It depicts the *agni-parīkṣā* (fire-ordeal) of Sītā, after she had been rescued in Laṅkā (Fig. 1.19). It is in what is known as the 'Popular Mughal' style, and is ascribable to circa 1610 CE.

4. Sculptural Representation of Rāma's Life-story Abroad

Earlier in this chapter we dealt with the literary evidence about the story of Rāma in various countries outside India. Here we take up the presentation of that story through the medium of sculptures. However, we shall present only two examples, one from Cambodia and the other from Indonesia.

Fig. 1.20 shows a scene from the famous temple at Ankor Vat, Cambodia. It is very intricately carved and within the carvings is set a scene which depicts Rāvaṇa carrying Sītā away, after abducting her. The temple is ascribable to the 11th century CE.

Prāmbanam, in Indonesia, has a 9th century temple which is full of scenes from the life-story of Rāma. The panel presented here (Fig. 1.21) shows Rāma subduing the sea. He holds an outstretched bow in his left hand. The sea is depicted by means of wavy lines and from within it crocodiles push their snouts out, making the entire scene very graphic.

H. AN ANALYSIS OF THE ENTIRE EVIDENCE

Let us begin with a hypothesis that Rāma was not a real-life person but a figment of the imagination of a poet called

Fig. 1.20. Ankor Vat: A stone panel in the temple, showing Rāvaṇa carrying away Sītā. 11th century CE.

Vālmīki. We may then ask ourselves a question: "Do the various kinds of evidences, namely those of literature, archaeology and art, presented in the preceding pages uphold such a hypothesis or controvert it?"

1. The Evidence of Literature

We shall first take up the literary data. Since Vālmīki himself has been put in the dock, we shall completely ignore his *Rāmāyaṇa*. Likewise, the other versions of the *Rāmāyaṇa* available from almost every part of the country, and even from abroad, may be put on the back burner since most of these drew their inspiration from the story contained in the *Rāmāyaṇa* of Vālmīki. But then what do we do with the **evidence of the Buddhist and Jain literature?** Why should these follow the dictates of the Brāhmaṇical (commonly called Hindu) texts? There wasn't any compulsion. But quite

Fig. 1.21. Prāmbanam, Indonesia: A scene from the temple depicting the subduing of sea by Rāma. 9th century CE.

independently of the Brāhmaṇical *Rāmāyaṇa* of Vālmīki, the *Jātaka*s, which constitute an important part of the Buddhist literature, do narrate the life-story of Rāma. Thus, for example, **in the famous *Daśaratha Jātaka* there is a clear mention of Rāma,** as well as of Lakṣmaṇa and Bharata. Also, there are many other details in the said *Jātaka*: for instance, the visit of Bharata to meet his brother Rāma while the latter was in exile, in order to communicate to him the news of the passing away of their father, Daśaratha, and to request Rāma to return to Ayodhyā and take over the reigns of the government. Without any expression of shock at the unpleasant news, Rāma asked Bharata to return to Ayodhyā, giving the latter his sandals as his symbol. **Why should have the Buddhists included in their texts the life-story of Rāma in such great detail, unless they had accepted it is as a real-life happening?**

There are two other *Jātaka*s which deserve mention: 'The *Jātaka* of the Unnamed King' and 'The *Nidāna* of the king of Ten Luxuries'. Though the originals are lost, their translations still exist in the Chinese language. The former was translated in 251 CE and the latter in 472 CE.

In this context it also needs to be emphasized that the period of the composition of the *Jātaka*s is almost the same as that of the *Rāmāyaṇa* of Vālmīki. In other words, it may mean that both these drew inspiration from an earlier narration, perhaps in the form of a ballad which was being sung over the centuries prior to the composition of these texts.

All this serves to emphasize how popular the life-story of Rāma was even amongst the Buddhists. Doubtless there are some variations in the details, but this would have been so because there was a great time-lag between the actual happenings and their narration in the Buddhist texts.

More telling than the foregoing is the **evidence of a purely secular, non-religious text, namely the *Arthaśāstra* of Kauṭilya, ascribable to the 4th century** BCE. This book is completely independent of the *Rāmāyaṇa* of Vālmīki. We have already furnished the details available from the relevant portions of the *Arthaśāstra* (above, pp. 14-15) and would thus recall here only the essentials.

The first *Adhikaraṇa* of the *Arthaśāstra*, deals with 'Discipline' and the sixth *Adhyāya* thereof with 'The Shaking off of the Aggregate of the Six Enemies'. In it Kauṭilya advises that one should not succumb to the following six enemies, namely *kāma* (lust), *krodha* (anger), *lobha* (greed), *māna* (vanity), *mada* (haughtiness) and *harṣa* (overjoy). After that he cites examples of kings and other personalities who in the past met their doom by having become a prey to one or the other of these evils. Amidst the narrations that follow, Kauṭilya says:

Mānādrāvaṇaḥ paradārānaprayachchhan;
Duryodhano rājyādaṁśam cha,

which means **"Rāvaṇa [perished because he was] unwilling, under the influence of vanity, to restore a stranger's wife, and so also Duryodhana [because he too was unwilling] to part with a portion of his kingdom".** The reference in the second anecdote is clearly to the *Mahābhārata* story wherein Duryodhana refused to give even an inch of the land to the Pāṇḍavas. In the first part of the same quotation,

'the wife of a stranger', who was 'not restored by Rāvaṇa' is definitely none other than Sītā. Thus, though Rāma is not specifically mentioned by Kauṭilya (and there was indeed no need for him to do so in the given context), the historicity of Rāma gets *ipso facto* established.

2. The Evidence of Archaeological Excavations

As mentioned earlier, in the late 1970s and early 1980s I took up a field-project named 'Archaeology of the Rāmāyaṇa Sites'. Under it five sites were excavated, namely: Ayodhyā, the birth-place of Rāma; Śṛiṅgaverapura, where Rāma, Sītā and Lakṣmaṇa crossed the the Gaṅgā during their exile; Bharadvāja Āśrama, where the trio spent a while to pay their respects to sage Bharadvāja; Chitrakūṭa where, during the trio's stay, Bharata came to persuade Rāma to return to Ayodhyā; and Nandīgrāma, from where Bharata carried on the government during the absence of Rāma.

The lowest cultural deposits common to all these sites were characterized by the Northern Black Polished Ware (NBPW) whose other associated features have also been described in the preceding pages. On the basis of the Carbon-14 dates provided by the Birbal Sahni Institute of Palaeobotany, Lucknow, the duration of the NBPW period at Ayodhyā ranges from somewhere in the 13th century BCE to about the 4th century BCE. While the presence of the NBPW at all these sites does no doubt tie them up in a common knot, this by itself is no proof of the historicity of the *Rāmāyaṇa*.

In this context, however, the evidence of Bharadvāja Āśrama is most revealing. There is no mound at the site: it is an entirely flat piece of land. Thus, no one could have ever imagined that it contained ancient remains. At the same time, there is a strong local tradition which associates the place with the sage Bharadvāja. I said to myself that if there was even an iota of truth in this local tradition, the site must bring forth remains of the same period as were met with at Ayodhyā. I dug about half-a-dozen trenches through this flat piece of land

and to my great surprise found structures of the Gupta period right below the surface. And as we went down, we encountered the Northern Black Polished Ware in the lower levels. But there was an amazing difference between the NBPW-yielding strata at Ayodhyā and those at Bharadvāja Āśrama. Whereas at Ayodhyā there were successive floors and overlying occupational deposits, at Bharadvāja Āśrama there were no floors nor regular occupational levels. On the other hand, what we met with there was a thick deposit of sandy loam within which sherds of the NBPW were found only sporadically. Also found in the loam were some pieces of clay bearing reed-impressions. Thus, the picture presented by the site was that of a very casual occupation in which mud-huts were the only structures. In earlier pages I dealt with the evidence which showed that the Gaṅgā flowed past this site, though now it has shifted its course a bit away. All this fits very well into a scenario of an *āśrama* on the bank of the Gaṅgā. But on the question whether the presiding sage over here was Bharadvāja or not, archaeology remains mute.

Here we must recall that the *Rāmāyaṇa* of Vālmīki was composed some time between the 3rd century BCE and 3rd century CE. During this period Bharadvāja Āśrama was not under occupation and thus not a 'living' entity. Then how could the poet include it into his narrative? This could have been possible only if there was an earlier story, carried down the generations in the form a ballad or some such device, which was reduced to writing in the form of the *Rāmāyaṇa*. **In other words, the *Rāmāyaṇa* was not a figment of the imagination of the poet but was based on a true story carried down over the centuries by word of mouth.** Earlier (pp. 32ff.) I cited two modern examples wherein true events – one dealing with the catastrophe during the 1954 Kumbha Melā at Allahabad and the other with the ghastly murder of a brother by his sister for the sake of money – have been incorporated in ballads that are being sung ever since. If in modern times, when we already have the print and electronic media, people do compose ballads based on contemporary events, why should one doubt there having been an oral tradition about the life-events of Rāma, perhaps carried down generation after generation in the form of a ballad and later on, when writing came to be used frequently, incorporated in the epic called the *Rāmāyaṇa*?

3. The evidence of Art

Delineation of the life-story of Rāma through the medium of art is no less telling. We have already discussed in great detail this topic (above, pp. 34 ff.) and hence here we shall confine ourselves only to some salient aspects. As stated earlier, three different media had been used for the purpose, namely terracottas, stone sculptures and paintings. Though all these are in vogue even today, in earlier periods only clay and stone media seem to have dominated. In so far as the representation of the story of Rāma in stone is concerned we may recall the exuberant sculptures from Nāgārjunakoṇḍā in Andhra Pradesh (3rd century CE), Nāchanā-Kuṭhārā in Madhya Pradesh (5th century CE) and Paṭṭadakala in Karnataka (7th-8th century CE). No less remarkable are the portrayals of Rāma's life outside India, e.g. at Prāmbanam in Indonesia (9th century CE) and at Ankor Vat in Cambodia (11th century CE).

However, for our present discussion more noteworthy are the delineations of the life of Rāma in terracotta. In this context, we may first recall the two pieces, one from Nachāra Kherā in Haryana portraying the visit of Rāma and Sītā to Pañchavaṭī (Fig. 1.12) and the other from Jind, also in Haryana, delineating the destruction of the Aśoka Vāṭikā in Laṅka by Hanumān (Fig. 1.14). Both these plaques bear supporting inscriptions in the Brāhmī characters of circa 4th century CE.

As we get back in time, **we have a very crucial terracotta, representing Rāma himself (Fig. 1.11). Executed in the art-style of the Kushan period, it also bears the name, Rāma, in Brāhmī characters of the 3rd century** CE. Currently, it is lodged in the LA County Museum of Art, USA, but is said to have come from Nachāra Kherā in Haryana. At this site there is a sizeable mound, perhaps concealing a brick temple devoted to Rāma.

Finally we shall refer to **a terracotta from Kauśāmbī in Uttar Pradesh. Ascribable to circa 2nd century BCE, it depicts a scene in which Sītā, after her abduction, is being carried away by Rāvaṇa**. She is throwing her ornaments down on the ground in the hope these may be picked up by some one, leading ultimately to her whereabouts (Fig. 1.10).

As just noted, this last-named terracotta, presenting a scene from the life-story of Rāma, belongs to circa 2nd century BCE. This is just the time when the idea of presenting the life-story of Buddha had also emerged, as exemplified by the scenes depicted at Sāñchī and Bharhut. A simple question may now be asked: **When on the basis of the scenes depicted at Sāñchī and Bharhut, we take as real the various episodes in the life of Buddha, why shouldn't we accept as real the life-story of Rāma as portrayed in the art of the same period?** Please think coolly and you will yourselves get the answer.

4. Must a Contemporary Inscription be the Sole Adjudicator of Rāma's Historicity?

A couple of paragraphs earlier we discussed the importance of the terracotta figure of Rāma which bears his name in Brāhmī characters of the 3rd century CE. But this does not seem to satisfy a certain class of persons as evidence enough of his historicity. They insist that unless we present to them an inscription contemporaneous with his life-time certifying his existence they would not accept that he was a real-life person. But have these persons ever cared to ponder over the fall-out of such a demand?

First of all, these persons ought to know that we have not come across any inscription prior to circa third century BCE. So, how can we expect to find an inscription

contemporary with Rāma who must have lived somewhere around 1000 BCE, as indicated by the Carbon-14 dates from Ayodhyā?

Secondly, let it be squarely stated that if a contemporary inscription is going to be the sole adjudicator of the historicity of Rāma, then, I am afraid, we will have to treat as non-historical even the two other religious leaders of ancient India, namely Buddha and Mahāvira, since in their cases too there is no contemporary inscription. Speaking of Buddha, the position is as follows. During the course of his tours, Emperor Ashok visited a place called Lumbini where the local inhabitants told him that Buddha's mother, while on way to her parents' place, gave birth to the child over there. On this hearsay, Ashok issued a pillar-edict, stating *hida budhe jate*, i.e. Buddha was born here (and consequently he reduced the quantum of taxes levied on the region). But let us not forget that there is a clear gap of over 300 years between the date of birth of Buddha and the time when Ashok visited Lumbini. **By no stretch of imagination can the Lumbini inscription be regarded as a 'contemporary' document.** In the case of Mahāvira, the position is much worse. There was no Ashok to issue, as it were, a 'birth-certificate'. In fact, any inscriptional evidence relating to Mahāvira is very much later.

Thus, the only sane thing to do is to take a holistic view of the entire available evidence, be it in the form of literature or archaeology or art. Absence of a contemporary inscription certifying Rāma's birth cannot be construed as evidence of his not having existed in flesh and blood. Thus goes the wise old saying: "Absence of evidence is no evidence of absence."

[CHAPTER II]

Was there a Temple in the Janma-bhūmi Area at Ayodhyā Preceding the Construction of the Babari Masjid?

As mentioned earlier (pp. 20ff.), excavations were carried out in the Janma-Bhūmi area at Ayodhyā as a part of the project 'Archaeology of the Rāmāyaṇa Sites'. Of the trenches laid out in this area, one was immediately to the south of and almost parallel to the boundary wall of the Babari Masjid, the intermediary space being hardly four metres. The lowest levels in this trench were characterized by an early stage of Northern Black Polished Ware, and on the basis of the Carbon-14 dates provided by the Birbal Sahni Research Institute of Palaeobotany, Lucknow, the beginning of the settlement at Ayodhyā would appear to go back to the last quarter of the 2nd millennium BCE.

In the uppermost levels of this trench, hardly 50 centimetres below the surface, were encountered rows of pillar-bases, squarish on plan and made of brick-bats sometimes intermixed with a few stones. While most of these bases were well within the trench, a few of them lay underneath the edge of the trench towards the boundary wall of the Masjid (Fig. 2.1). Associated with the pillar-base-complex there were successive floors made of lime mixed with brick jelly. No coin or inscription was found on these floors but on the basis of the associated pottery and other antiquities the entire complex could be dated from the twelfth to fifteenth century CE.

Attached to the piers of the Babari Masjid there were twelve stone pillars which carried not only typical Hindu motifs and mouldings but also figures of Hindu deities (Figs. 2.3 and 2.4). It was self-evident that these pillars were not an integral part of the Masjid but were foreign to it. Since, as already stated, the pillar-bases were penetrating into the Masjid-complex, a question naturally arose whether these bases had anything to do with the above-mentioned pillars affixed to the piers of the Masjid.

A summary report on the essentials of the excavations at Ayodhyā was published in *Indian Archaeology 1976-77 – A Review*, pp. 52-53. Since the main objective of the excavation was to ascertain the antiquity of the settlement, the brief report in the *Review* did not make any mention of these pillar-bases. In fact, these had nothing to do with the main enquiry.

However, since these pillar-bases raised a question about their relationship with the pillars affixed to the piers of the Masjid, which evidently had originally belonged to a Hindu temple, these did draw public attention. The first reaction that came up from a certain category of historians was to deny the very existence of these pillar-bases. Their approach was simple: if there were no pillar-bases, the question of their relationship with the pillars affixed to the piers of the Babari Masjid became automatically redundant. These historians took recourse to publishing all sorts of unsavoury comments in the newspapers. However, when they were told that the pillar-bases were not someone's fantasy but their photographs (along with the negatives), taken at the time of the excavation, did exist in the photo-archives of the Excavations Branch of the Archaeological Survey of India, they gave up their first exercise in denial, of which more would be said later.

Then came up a brilliant brain-wave from a professor of the University of Allahabad, who published a book on the

Fig. 2.1. Ayodhyā: View of a trench in the Janma-Bhūmi area, showing pillar-bases constructed of brick-bats with occasional use of stones.

Fig. 2.2. An archaeologist tries to deny the individual identity of the pillar-bases by drawing a black line along their right-hand edges and thereby calling them a 'wall'.

Fig. 2.3. Ayodhyā: A pillar of the pre-existing 12th century Hindu temple, re-fixed against a pier of the Babari Masjid.

Fig. 2.4. Ayodhyā: Another pillar of the pre-existing Hindu temple, re-fixed against yet another pier of the Babari Masjid.

issue. He drew on the photograph a black line along the right-hand edges of the pillar-bases and asserted that these constituted a 'wall' and thus tried to deny their nature as pillar-bases. Wrote he (Mandal 1994, p. 36):

> It is suggested here that the features designating rows of 'pillar bases' in the excavated trench under discussion are actually the remains of the walls of rooms, and not pillars.

Fig. 2.2, a true copy of Mandal's reconstruction (Pl. III of his book), clearly shows the manipulation involved.

In this context, it may also be well worth narrating an incident. Those days I was staying in the Guest House in Purana Qila, New Delhi, in connection with the preparation of the report on Śṛiṅgaverapura. One night, after I had retired to bed, I heard a knock at the door. When I opened the door I was surprised to see the familiar face of a professor from the University of Kurukshetra. I welcomed him and offered a cup of tea. He told me that he had been to Ayodhyā and had physically verified the pillar-bases but wanted to check up the field-drawings. I told him that the drawings were in the office and I would be able show the same to him only the following morning. Annoyed, he left the guest house. Next morning what I read in the newspapers was a **statement by this professor that while there did exist the pillar-bases in the Janma-Bhūmi area, these belonged to a cow-shed.** What an ingenious thesis to explain away the purpose of these bases which were associated with successive floors, made of a fine combination of lime and brick-jelly! In this context it needs to be added that, after a recent order of the Lucknow Bench of the Allahabad High Court, the **Archaeological Survey of India** carried out excavation in the area which earlier lay underneath the Babari Masjid and **has discovered that the series of pillar-bases continues all over the area. What kind of a cow-shed does this learned professor envisage now ?**

In 1991, the Museums Association of India invited me to deliver a talk on my excavations at Ayodhyā. The venue was Vijayawada and the date the 10th of February. After my lecture was over, the scholars present there asked me if there were more pillar-bases underneath the Babari Masjid and what was the relationship between the pillar-bases met with in the excavation and the pillars of a Hindu temple affixed to the piers of the Masjid. More pointedly, they wanted me tell them if there was any temple underneath the mosque. Not being a sooth-sayer, I replied, as any archaeologist would do, that unless excavations were carried out in the area concerned, it was not possible to arrive at any conclusion. The area covered by the floor of the Masjid was quite wide and it was possible to do a few probes, without damaging the structure. But no one cared to listen to my suggestion.

Curiously, events take their own course. On December 6, 1992, the Masjid was demolished by the Kar Sevaks who had assembled in a large number at the site. The demolition, though regrettable, brought to light a great deal of archaeological material from within the thick walls of the Masjid. From the published reports it is gathered that there were more than 200 specimens which included many sculptured panels and architectural components which must have once constituted parts of the demolished temple. Besides, there were three inscriptions, of which two are illustrated here (Figs. 2.5 and 2.6).

Of the above-mentioned three inscriptions, the largest one **is** engraved on a stone slab, measuring 1.10 x .56 metres, and consists of 20 lines (Fig. 2.5). It has since been published by Professor Ajaya Mitra Shastri of Nagpur University in the *Purātattva,* No. 23 (1992-93), pp. 35 ff. (Professor Shastri, who unfortunately is no more, was a distinguished historian and a specialist in Epigraphy and Numismatics.) The relevant part of his paper reads as follows:

> The inscription is composed in high-flown Sanskrit verse, except for a small portion in prose, and is engraved in the chaste and classical Nāgarī script of the eleventh-twelfth

Fig. 2.5. A 1.10 x .56 metre stone slab carrying a 20-line long inscription. Written in characters of the 12th century CE, it gives all the details regarding the construction of the temple.

century AD. It has yet to be fully deciphered, but the portions which have been fully deciphered and read are of great historical significance for our purpose here. It was evidently put up on the wall of the temple, the construction of which is recorded in the text inscribed on it. Line 15 of this inscription, for example, clearly tells us that a beautiful temple of Vishṇu-Hari, built with heaps of stone (*śilā-saṁhati-grahais*) and beautified with a golden spire (*hiraṇya-kalaśa-śrisundaram*) unparalleled by any other temple built by earlier kings

Fig. 2.6. Another inscription, on a pillar, recovered from within the walls of the Babari Masjid.

(*pūrvvair-apy-akṛitam kṛitam nṛipatibhir*) was constructed. This wonderful temple (*aty-adbhutam*) was built in the temple-city (*vibudh-ālayānī*) of Ayodhyā situated in the Sāketamaṇḍala (district, line 17) showing that Ayodhyā and Sāketa were closely connected, Sāketa being the district of which Ayodhyā was a part. Line 19 describes god Vishṇu as destroying king Bali (apparently in the Vāmana manifestation) and **the ten-headed personage (*Daśānana* i.e. Rāvaṇa).**

The inscription makes it abundantly clear that there did exist at the site a temple datable to circa 11th-12th century CE. The sculptures and inscribed slab that came out from within the walls of the Masjid belonged to this very temple.

It has been contented by certain historians that these images, architectural parts and the inscribed slab were brought by the Kar Sevaks from somewhere else and surreptitiously placed there at the time of the demolition of the Masjid. This contention is absolutely baseless. Transportation of the above-mentioned material from elsewhere would have required the use of many trucks, an act which would have certainly been noticed by the innumerable representatives of the print and electronic media present on the spot to cover the event. On the other hand, a reputed journal, *India Today*, published in its issue dated December 31, 1992 a photograph (here Fig. 2.7) which shows the Kar Sevaks carrying on their shoulders a huge stone-slab sculpted with a long frieze, after having picked it up from the debris.

The above-mentioned historians have also alleged that the inscription has been forged. This is behaving like the Village School Master of Oliver Goldsmith, who, 'though vanquished would argue still'. So many eminent epigraphists of the country have examined the inscribed slab and not even one of them is of the view that the inscription is forged. Anyway, to allay any misgivings, I append here a Note from the highest authority on epigraphical matters in

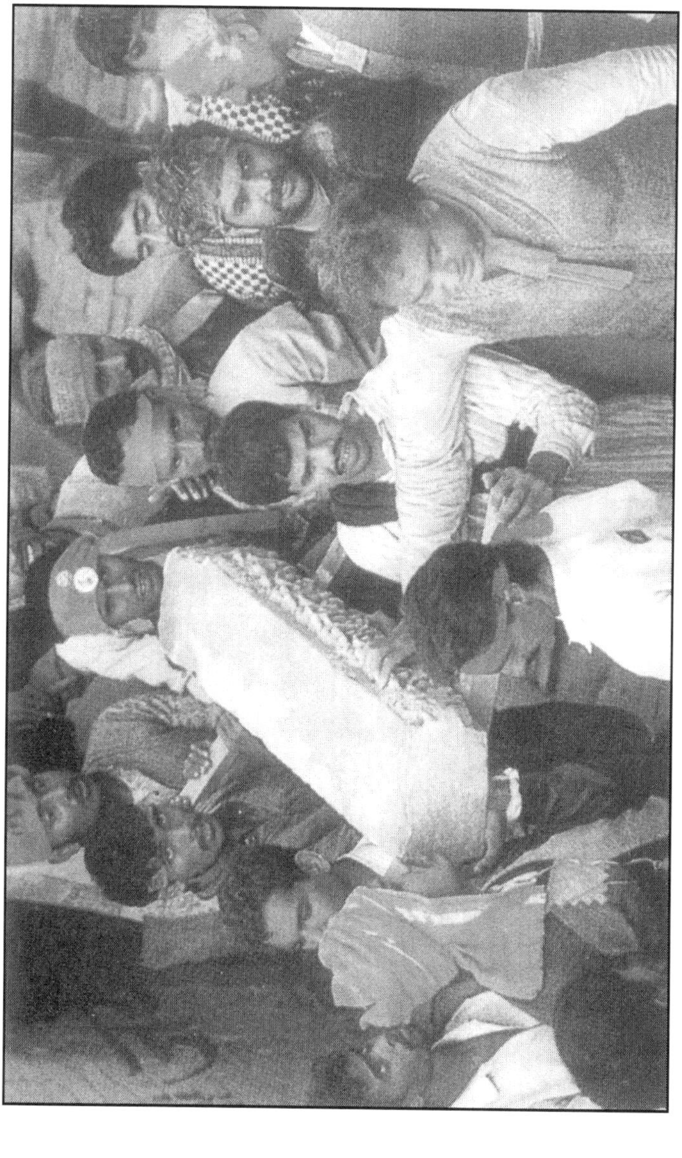

Fig. 2.7. Kar Sevaks carrying a huge sculpted stone-slab on their shoulders, which they had rescued from the debris of the Masjid and were in the process of depositing it in a safe place.

the country, namely the Director of Epigraphy, Archaeological Survey of India, Dr. K.V. Ramesh (Appendix II). In it he first gives a summary of the inscription, then an actual reading of the text and finally an English translation thereof. While scholars would certainly like to go through the Note, it may straightaway be stated here that according to it this temple was built by Meghasuta who obtained the lordship of Sāketa-maṇḍala [i.e. the Ayodhyā region] through the grace of a senior Lord of the earth, viz. Govinda Chandra of the Gahaḍavāla dynasty, who ruled over a vast empire, from 1114 to 1155 CE.

In this entire context, it also needs to be added that there exist hundreds of examples, all over the country, of the destruction of temples and incorporation of their material in the mosques during the mediaeval times. **For example, right in Delhi there is the Quwwatu'l-Islam Mosque ('Might of Islam') near the Qutb Minar, which incorporated parts of a large number of temples that had been wantonly destroyed by Qutub-ud-din Aibak.** Fig. 2.8 shows, standing within the mosque complex, a colonnade which was constructed by using sculpted pillars of the demolished 27 Hindu and Jain temples. This was a matter of glory for the conqueror as has been recorded by himself in an inscription still existing on inner lintel of the eastern entrance of the mosque (Fig. 2.9). Its English translation, by Maulvi Zafar Hasan, is as follows:

> This fort was conquered and this Jami Masjid was built in (the months of) the year 587 [1191-92 AD] by the Amir, the great and glorious commander of the army, (named) Qutb-ud-daulat-wa-d-dīn, the Amir-ul-umara Aibak Sultani, may God strengthen his helpers. **The material of 27 temples, on (the erection of) each of which 2,000,000 Deliwals had been spent, were used in (the construction of) this mosque.** May God the great and glorious have mercy on him who should pray for the faith of the founder of the good (building).

Fig. 2.8. Constituting a part of the Quwwatu'l-Islam (Might of Islam) Mosque in Delhi is the above colonnade. It was constructed by using pillars of Hindu and Jain temples destroyed by Qutub-ud-din Aibak.

(*a*) Qutb Mosque (Masjid Quwwatul Islam).
(*b*) Immediately to N. E. of the Qutb Minar.
(*c*) Government.
(*d*) Ia.
(*e*) 587 A. H. (1191 A. D.).
(*f*) On the inner lintel of the eastern gateway.

Quran, Sura III, verses 91-2 followed by the inscription given below —

این حصار را فتح کرد و این مسجد جامع را بساخت بتاریخ في شهور سنه سبع و ثمانین
و خمسمایة امیر اسفهسالار اجل کبیر قطب الدولة و الدین امیر الامرا ایبک سلطاني اعز الله
انصاره بیست و هفت الت بتخانه که در هر بتخانه دو بار هزار بار هزار دلیوال صرف شده بود درین
مسجد بکار بسته شده است خدائی عزوجل بران بنده رحمت کند هر که بر نیت باني خیر دعا
ایمان گوید .

Fig. 2.9. Transcript of an inscription on the lintel of the eastern gate of the Quwwatu'l-Islam Mosque, Delhi. It refers to the demolition of 27 temples whose material was used in the construction of the mosque.

To sum up. The evidence presented in the foregoing paragraphs in respect of the existence of a Hindu temple in the Janma Bhūmi area at Ayodhyā preceding the construction of the Babari Masjid is so eloquent that no further comments are necessary. Unfortunately, the basic problem with a ceratin category of historians and archaeologists – and others of the same ilk – is that seeing they see not or knowingly they ignore. Anyway, in spite of them the truth has revealed itself.

CHAPTER III

What are the 'Credentials' of the Rāma Setu?

Starting from Dhanushkodi, located on the sea-shore in Tamil Nadu on the Indian side, there runs in an east-southeasterly direction a chain of sandbanks, underlain by coral reefs and limestone shoals, right up to Talaimannar on the Mannar island, a northern part of Sri Lanka. The stretch is about 30 kilometres in length (Figs. 3.1, 3.2, 3.3 and 3.4). This chain is known as the Rāma Setu as well as Adam's Bridge. At present, some of these sandbanks are above the sea-level and some others are submerged. But a map assignable to the 16th-17th century CE shows a land-link between India and Sri Lanka, naming it as Pont d'Adam i.e Adam's Bridge. An account published in the Gazetteer of Ramanathapuram District of Tamil Nadu also refers to the Rāma Setu (*Sethu Palam*). It is held that up to 1480 CE this land-link functioned as a bridge between India and Sri Lanka. This is stated to be based on certain-records. I have tried to verify it but have not succeeded so far. Anyway, back in the 13th century CE, the Venetian traveller **Marco Polo** visited many parts of the world and refers to this feature as '**Setabund Rameshwara**' (i.e. a *Setu* = bridge, related to Rāma). In the 11th century CE, **Alberuni** gave the following account of the Rāma Setu (*Alberuni's India*, edited by Edward C. Sachau, Vol. I, Chapter XVIII, p. 209, reprinted by S. Chand & Co., Delhi): "The next place on the coast is Ūmmalnāra, then Rāmsher

Fig. 3.1. An Overview of the Rāma Setu (Adam's Bridge) between India and Sri Lanka.

(Rameshar?) opposite Sarandīb (Ceylon); the distance of the sea between them is 12 *farsakh*. The distance from Panjayāvar to Ramsher is 40 *farsakh*, that between Rāmsher and **Setubandha** 2 *farsakh*. **Setubandha** means **bridge of the ocean**. It is the dike of **Rāma, the son of Daśaratha**, which he built from the continent to the castle Laṅkā. At present it consists

Fig. 3.2. Close-up of the Rāma Setu (Adam's Bridge) between India and Sri Lanka.

Fig. 3.3. Close-up of a part the Rāma Setu, showing its firm edges on both the sides, which is suggestive of human agency.

of isolated mountains between which the ocean flows." Going all the way back, in the 3rd century BCE Ashok, after his adoption of Buddhism, wanted to propagate that religion. As a part this exercise, he sent his son, Mahendra, and daughter,

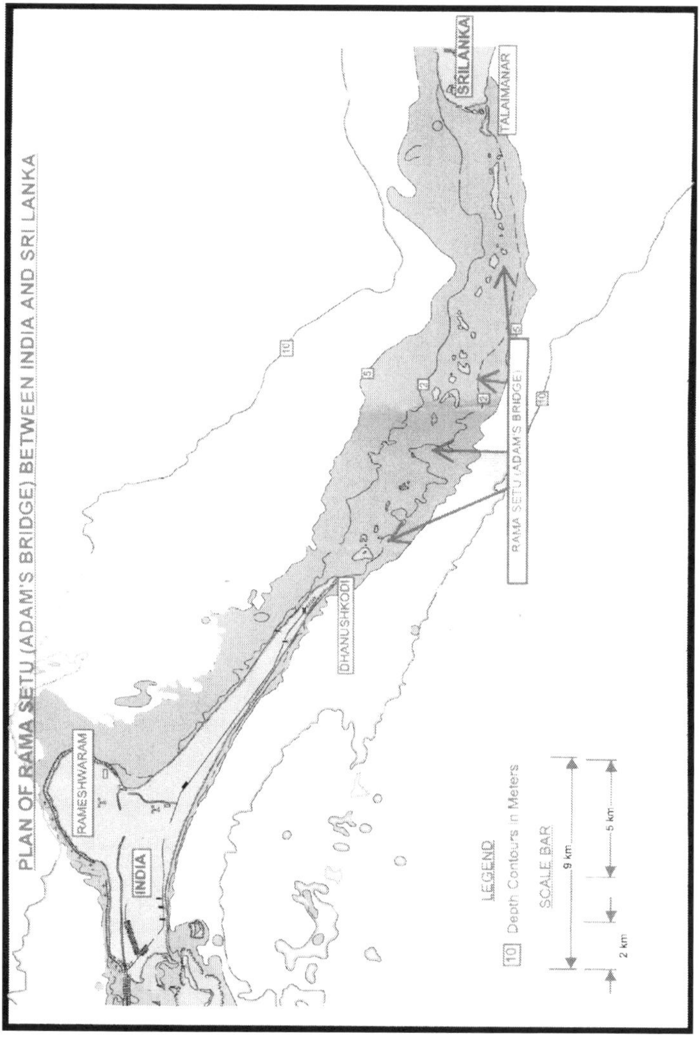

Fig. 3.4. Plan of the Rāma Setu (Adam's Bridge) between India and Sri Lanka.

Sanghamitra, to Sri Lanka. They carried with them a branch of the pipal tree from Bodh Gaya, under which Buddha had achieved enlightenment. It is held by some scholars that they took a land-route to Sri Lanka. If that be so, it could have been only this bridge.

Evidences of inscriptions and coins, which leave little scope for any ambiguity, also point to the existence of the Rāma Setu in ancient times. Thus, for example, **the Hampi inscription of Kṛiṣṇadevarāya, dated to 1508 CE, refers many times to the Rāma Setu.** Just as nowadays, while referring to the extent of our country, we use the expression *'Kashmir se Kanyākumārī taka'* (i.e. 'from Kashmir to Kanyākumārī', both of which are realities) in ancient times the phrase used in such a context was *'hemāchalāntādāsetor'* i.e. 'from the golden mountain (Meru) to the Setu'. One such reference in the above-mentioned inscription is quoted here:

> Seated on a jewelled throne at Vijayanagara, king Kṛiṣṇarāya, whose liberality was worthy to be praised by the learned, ... was resplendent with fame from the eastern mountains to the slopes of the mountain of the west **and from the mountain of gold (*Meru*) to (*Rāma's*) Bridge.**

The insertion of the word 'Rāma's' in the foregoing translation is by **E. Hultzsch** who published the inscription in *Epigraphia Indica,* Volume I, **in 1892**. He was convinced that the **'Setu'** referred to was none other than the **'Rāma Setu'**. He never dreamt that more than a century later there would be a debate about the identification of '**the** Setu'.

Likewise, the **coins** issued by the Tamil kings of Nallur in Jafna, who ruled from the 13th to 17th century CE, affirm the existence of the Rāma Setu, in the same manner as does the foregoing inscription. One such coin is illustrated here. It bears a human figure on the obverse, while on the reverse there is a sitting *nandī* (bull, the vehicle of Śiva) with a crescent-moon above it and the word ***'Setu'*** in Tamil below it (Fig. 3.5). It may, incidentally, be noted that this numismatic evidence comes not from the Indian side but from Sri Lanka.

Fig. 3.5. A Setu Bull Coin; the reverse of the Setu Bull Coin.

While the above-noted evidences of literature, tradition, cartography, epigraphy and numismatics have their own significance and value, I have chosen to make a purely scientific enquiry into the matter in order to find out if there could have at all existed a land-connection between Dhanushkodi and Talaimannar in ancient times. The first part of my investigation was to prepare a cross-section of the Rāma Setu, as it exists now, right from the Indian side to its end in Sri Lanka, with the present sea-level as the datum-line. The result is presented here in the form a line-drawing at Fig. 3.6. It would be seen that many of the sandbanks are even today above the sea-level. However, what is no less important is that even in the stretches where no sandbanks are seen **the depth of the sea is generally between 0.5 and 1 metre, but in no case more than 1.5 metres.**

The next step was to find out the behaviour of the sea-level in antiquity. It is well known that out of the total amount of water on our planet a part is locked up in the form of the snow and the remaining flows in the sea. Further, when there is an intensely cold period, the quantum of snow becomes more and that of the water in the sea gets reduced. Geologists and palaeo-climatologists have worked out this behavoiur and have come to the conclusion that there have been at least four major Glacial Periods in the past, namely Gunz, Mindel, Riss and Wurm. Each time there was a Glacial Period there was a corresponding lowering down of the sea-level. Likewise, with each warm period, technically named as the Inter-glacial Period, there was a rise of the sea-level.

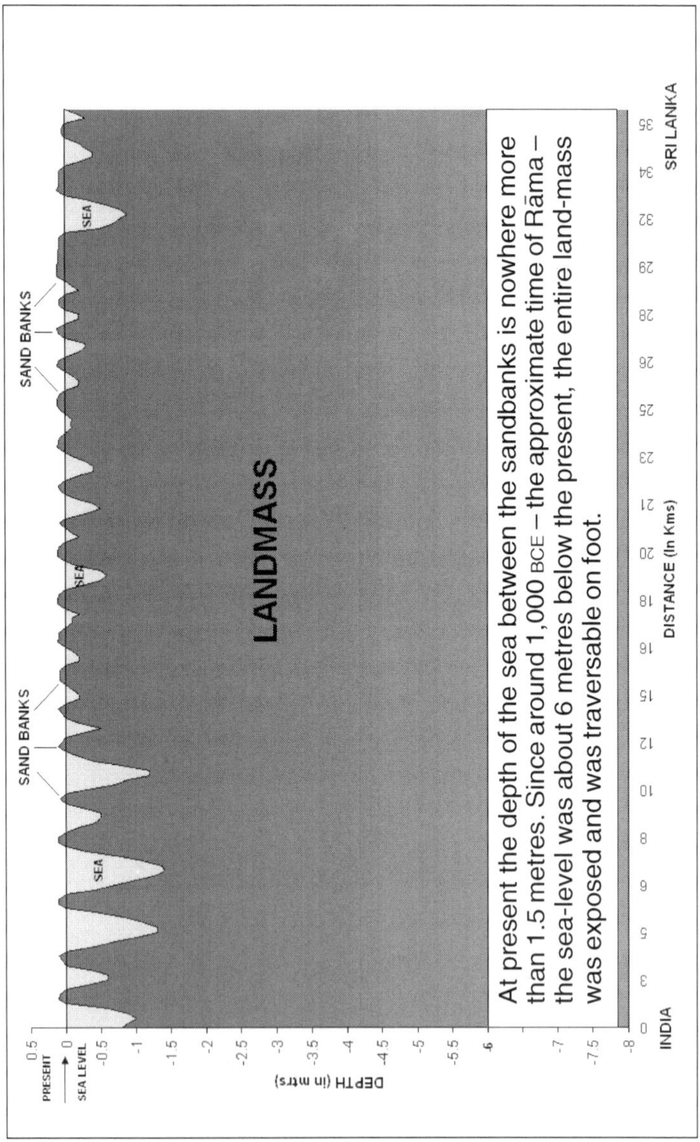

Fig. 3.6. Cross-section of the Rāma Setu (Adam's Bridge).

The last glacial period is known to have ended around 10,000 years ago. Thereafter began the what is known as the Holocene. With the gradual warming up of the climate there began the melting of the snow and consequent rise of the sea-level. Scientists have worked on the quantum of this rise. While they all agree that there has been a rise in the sea-level since the beginning of the Holocene, their estimates vary. Here I shall quote three of these, representing the maximum down to the minimum. Thus, Nair and Hashimi (1988: 83-86) hold:

> Radiocarbon-dated samples of shallow water origin from the western shelf indicate a low stand of sea-level between 90 and 100 metres about 10,000 years ago. From the lack of evidence of still-stands on a submerged shelf edge reef and from coral growth rates, it is inferred that sea level rose at the rate of 10m/1,000 years on the western continental margin of India.

According to another estimate, in circa 8,000 BCE the sea-level may have been 60 metres below the present, while during the period between 4,000 and 5,000 BCE it may have been around 17 metres below the present. The most conservative estimate holds that there has been a rise of 2mm per year, which makes it only 2 metres per 1,000 years. Anyway, what does become evident is that because of the warming up of the climate the sea-level has indeed been rising.

The implications of the rise of the sea-level since the beginning of the Holocene around 10,000 years ago are very interesting on a world-wide basis too. Says a scientific study (*Microsoft Encarta 2006*):

> Global sea-level was at least 30 metres below the present level about 10,000 years ago due to the large amounts of water still held on land in remnant ice sheets. **The final melting of the ice sheets, called the Flandrian Transgression, ... caused the separation of Ireland from the mainland of Great Britain and of Great Britain from mainland Europe.**

If such drastic has been the story of the submergence of land-connections in Europe, why should it be surprising if a similar phenomenon took place in respect of the land-link between the southern tip of India and the northern tip of Sri Lanka ?

In this context it may be added that archaeological excavations at coastal sites in various parts of the world have also confirmed a rise in the sea-level. Thus, for example, while digging in 1945 at Arikamedu, an ancient sea-port near Pondicherry, we found that **the lower part of the Indo-Roman warehouse, ascribable to 1st-2nd century CE, is now below the sea-level (*Ancient India*, 1946, No. 2, Fig. 2, p. 23).**

To return to the case of the Rāma Setu. On a projection of even the **minimum** of the above-mentioned estimates, viz. 2 metres per 1,000 years, it would follow that around 1,000 BCE, the sea-level may have been at least 6 metres below the present. While discussing the results of the excavations at Ayodhyā we noted that, on the basis of the C-14 dates, the lower levels of the site are ascribable to a period from circa 1,200 BCE onwards (pp. 29-30). **Thus, the period of Rāma, whose historicity has already been discussed in the concluding part of Chapter I, would fall say around 1,000 BCE. Further, as already noted, at that point of time the sea-level must have been at least 6 metres below the present. Such a situation would have exposed the entire land-mass from Dhanushkodi to Talaimannar, as would be absolutely clear by having a second look at Fig. 3.6.** However, even assuming that an odd stretch here or there still contained some water, the same would have been very shallow. Hence it would have been easily possible to fill up these shallow stretches by digging parts of the exposed sandbanks and shoals and dumping the material into these patches and thus create a ford in order to cross over to Sri Lanka. **To achieve this, Rāma did not need a "graduate degree from an engineering college", as demanded by an eminent political figure of the country. Let us not lose our cool !**

Appendix I

A *VIRAHĀ* (BALLAD) DEALING WITH THE HUMAN TRAGEDY DURING THE *KUMBHA MELĀ* AT ALLAHABAD IN 1954

विरहा-१, भाग-१ (गंगा जी की स्तुति*)

सुमिरी सूरसती जग तारन, मइयाँ भूलि गइउ केहि कारन दहिने पे होइजा तइयार।

१. पहिले हम गाई गंगा जी के सुमिरनवाँ,
जउन गंगा मइया दिहिन नान्हे से गियनवाँ।
जिला है इलाहाबाद तासिल सोरमवाँ,
थाना है नबाबगंज राम चौरा है मकनवा।।
जउन गंगा मइया दिहिन नान्हे से गियनवाँ।।

२. उत्तर और पूरब के दुइ बाटइ मोहरवाँ,
द्वारे पे नारा वाटइ पीपर बा निसनवाँ।
जउन गंगा मइया दिहिन नान्हे से गियनवाँ।

३. अउर आगे गंगा जी के तट अहै बाबा के स्थनवा,
सिंगरौर देवी के धाम मेला लगइ करखा।
जउन गंगा मइया दिहिन नान्हे से गियनवाँ।
इधर से चला जोर से मेला उधर से लौटा सधुवन का रेला
इसी से बाँध के नीचे मचिगा घमसनवाँ ना।।
अंधा मगता लंगड़ा लूल गया सब का मांगना भूल

---

* The Hindi spellings are as per pronunciation of *viraha* singer.

बचे एक नहीं जम लोक का किहेन पयनवां ना।।
रेली रेला में गिर जाते उनको कोई नहीं उठवाते
हड्डी टूट-टूट के होई गइन पिसनवा।।
करावइ असननवाँ चली।।

४. घर के कितने नर औ नारी बच्चा लिए गोद महतारी,
देखा पल भर में दिहेन जान गबनवां ना
तब से हुकुम भवला सरकारी पहुंची जाई मलेटरी लारी
सब के भर के भेजै कोतवाली दरम्यनवाँ ना
लास की ढेर लगवाई जूता कपड़ा लिहेसि मंगवाई,
बर्तन हुवाँ पें गजिगा जैसे लाग दुकनवाँ ना।।
लास की फोटो खिचवाई घायल अस्पताल भिजवाई
भूले भटको का किहेसि ऐलनवा ना।।
कहते राम अधार ललकारी यह सब सारद की बलिहारी
करावइ स्ननवां चली।।

विरहा-१, भाग-२ (कुम्भ का कथन)

करूँ कुम्भ का खतन सन् रहा १९५४ माघ मेलवा में आवा तुफनवा करावइ स्ननवाँ चली।।

१. हुआ पहिले से शोर मेला होगा बटडा जोर
इसीसे पहिले से किहिन इन्तजमवाँ ना।।
पुलिस मलेटरी मंगवाई सड़क की दूकानें हटवाई,
खाई खंदक कइलेन सड़क के समनवाँ ना।।
पुल तो जघे-जघे बनवाई, टीका हैजे के लगवाई
गाड़ी छूटलि अहै जनता मेल तुफनवा ना।।
जमुना अरइल जी के पास जहाज का अड्डा बना है खास
वहां पे उतरइ लगो आइ के वायुयनवा ना।।
झूसी, बदरा, दारागंज, अलोपी, बैरहना एक रंग,
अरइल, कीट गंज ना खाली मैदनवा।।
करावइ स्ननवाँ चली।।

२. डेरा तम्बू गवा है लाग दशा गई वहाँ की जाग
अइसा कभउ न भवा प्रयाग में नहनवा ना।।
जब की तीन फरवरी आई दिनवा बुद्ध का रहा भाई
लोगये करइ चले कुम्भ स्ननवाँ ना।।
बांध के नीचे गढ्ढा भूखा मनई खाई-खाई के सूखा
कितने मरिगे नर औ नारी बूढ़ जवनवाँ ना।।

Appendix II

AYODHYĀ VIṢṆU-HARI TEMPLE INSCRIPTION

—K.V. Ramesh

The subjoined stone inscription is engraved on a rectangular stone slab, the written area roughly covering an area of 115 cms. X 55 cms. The slab as at present extant is diagonally broken in two leading to the loss of a couple of letters in almost every line. Besides, the first and last two lines have suffered heavy damage resulting in the loss of many letters. All in all, the loss of letters have proved a handicap to epigraphists and Sanskritists in the matter of fully interpreting the contents of the text. Nevertheless, the overall purport and the crux of its import are clear beyond doubt. In the first instance a hurriedly prepared estampage, and in recent times, a high quality estampage as well as some photographs were all provided by Dr. S.P. Gupta, Chairman, Archaeological Society of India, New Delhi for which I am highly thankful to him.

The text of the inscription is written in fairly chaste Sanskrit, the orthographical features being regular for the period to which the inscription belongs, namely the middle of the 12th century AD. The inscription is not in any way dated, but may be assigned, with confidence, to the middle of the 12th century on palaeographical grounds as well as the internal evidence provided by the inscriptional text in question.

But for the opening salutation to Śiva at the very beginning, the entire text of the inscription is composed in Sanskrit verse of fairly high literary excellence. As has been stated above, the palaeographical and orthographical features are normal for the period to which the inscription belongs, viz. the middle of the 12th century AD. This was an important period of transition from classical Sanskrit to the North Indian vernaculars. This can be easily identified in contemporaneous inscriptions, including the present one, in the confusion in the use of class nasals and *anusvāra*, and in the employment of the sibilants and palatals.

As for the contents of the text, it is fully reflective of medieval vanity as far as the eulogies of the heroes mentioned in the inscription are concerned. **The most important internal historical information we get from this epigraph is the mention of Govindachandra, obviously of the Gahadavala dynasty, who ruled over a fairly vast empire from AD 1114 to AD 1115.**

Verse 1 is entirely lost. Verse 2, which is badly mutilated, refers to Trivikrama and hence, may have been composed in praise of Lord Viṣṇu. Verse 3, which is also badly damaged, seems to allude to the near-total decimation of the warrior clans by Bhārgava-Paraśurāma. Verse 4 refers to the emergence of a Kṣatriya family, heroes born in which successfully resurrected the decadent warrior clans. According to verse 5, in that noble family was born the beloved of the people, Māme. Verse 7 speaks of his detachment from mundane things while verse 8 informs us that he bequeathed his realm and wealth to his son Sallakṣaṇa. Verses 9 to 14 contain conventional praises showered on this Sallakṣaṇa in which the poet has displayed a high level of poetic imagination. Verse 15 refers to the birth of his son whose stunning resemblance to his father was the talk among the people. Verse 16 refers to this son as Alhaṇa and credits him with retrieving the past power and glory of his family. While the next two verses (17 and 18) contain his conventional praise, **verse 19 gives the information that his nephew, Meghasuta by name, as superseding a certain Anayacandra and obtaining the Lordship of Saketa-**

maṇḍala through the grace of the senior lord of the earth, Govindacandra. While verse 20 lauds the military might of this hero, verse 21 gives the important information that, in order to ensure his easy passage into the heavens, **Meghasuta built a lofty stone temple for the God Viṣṇu-Hari.** From verse 22 we learn that he, who was responsible for the stability of Govindacandra's empire, was succeeded by the younger Āyuṣyacandra as the lord of Sāketa-maṇḍala. Verse 23 contains his conventional praise. According to verse 24, he set up residence in the city of Ayodhyā, which was adorned with lofty abodes, intellectuals and temples, and added to the entire Sāketa-maṇḍala thousands of small and big water reservoirs. Verses 25 and 26 contain more conventional praises of Āyuṣyacandra. Verse 27, which is partly damaged, alludes to the well-known episodes of Viṣṇu's incarnations as Narasiṃha, Kṛṣna, Vāmana and Rāma. The badly damaged verse 28 refers to a king (probably Āyuṣyacandra) as warding off the danger of invasion from the west (i.e., from the invading Muslim forces). Verse 29, which is incomplete, mentions the King Āyuṣyacandra.

The reference to Sāketa-maṇḍala is interesting. It is well known that North India, just as in the case of the South, was divided into administrave divisions called *maṇḍala*s (see the word *maṇḍala* in the indices to H.C. Ray's monumental two-volume work 'The Dynastic History of Northern India', II edn., 1973, Delhi.

TEXT

[Metres: verses 1(?), 2, 3, 4, 10, 13, 20, 21, 27, Śārdūlavikrīḍitam; verses 5, 6, 7, 17, 19, 24, 25, 28, Vasantatilakā; verse 8, Śikhariṇī; verses 9, 22, 23, 29 Upajāti; verses 11, 18, 26, Anuṣṭubh; verses 12, Hariṇī; verse 14, Śālinī; verse 16, Rathoddhatā; verse 15, Mālinī]

१. नमः शिवा[य] [II*] -- U U - U-U UU -- U - - - - UU- U - U U U- - - U
-- U - [I*] - - - U - U - U U U - - - U - - U - - - - U U - U - U U U - - - U
-- U - - - - U U - U - U U U - - - U - - U [II*1] - - - U U - स्-त्रिविक्रम-तनोर्-
आ - U - - U - प्रांशुत्वेन निखर्व्व-षो-

२. डश-समुद्देशांदधानस्तनुं [I]
संवर्त्त-प्रमद्-ओद्धत्त:कुलगिरि-ग्राव-प्रहार-क्वणद्-ब्रह्माण्डं करसंपुटेन
विधुवन्-मध्यो ह - - U - [II*2] द्धार्ग्गव वि U - U U U -
द्वंसो(शोऽ)वतंसो भुव: I यस्मिन्-रा-

३. U U - ल-संक्लिमिर्-इव स्थायिन्य्-उदंचद्-भुज - - श्व्-ओपचिते परार्थ-घटना वंध्य-आननं जज्ञिरे II [3*] ते चंडीपति-चंड-तांडव-चलच्-चूडा U - - U - ब्रह्मांड्-ओच्च-कपाल-रंध्र-सरणी-प्रस्थायि-सत्कीर्त्तय: I वीरास्-तत्र कुले जनिं जगृहि-

४. रे ये भार्ग्गवीय्-आहव-क्षीण-क्षत्रिय-शेष-रक्षण-विधौ (ब)द्धोऽभियोगग्रह: II[4*]
वंश्यन्-तद्-एव
कुलम्-आकुलता-निवृत्ति-निर्व्यूढम्-अप्रतिम-[विक्रम]-जन्मभूमि: I
यत्र-आतिसाहस-सहश्र(स्र)-समिद्ध-धामा मामेऽजनिष्ट जगद्-इष्टतम्-ओत्त-

५. मश्री: II[5*] मा मे दयास्तु वपुषि द्रविणेषु तृष्णा
निष्णातिर्-अप्य्-अविरसा सरसेंद्रिय्-अर्थे I इत्युद्धृणन्न्-अनुदिनं से
दिनेशवत्सो मोमे प - U जगदे जगदेक [वीर:] II[6*]
तद्-युद्धकेलि-दलित्-अखिल-मेद-भिल्ल-पल्ली-सहस्त्र-वनितासु निकुंजगासु I उत्कंट-

६. का विटपिनो विट-विष्टितानि ते स्वस्तनेषु जघनेषु मुहुर्-लिखंत: II[7*] पुरा कीर्त्त्या न्यस्तन्-तदनु तनुन्-आध्यासितुमना मनस्वी स्वर्ल्लोकं परिणतिम्-उपे[त्य्-आति]शयिनीं [I*] स सर्व्वस्वं क्षत्रं क इव भुवि सल्लक्षण-सुते श्रिया सार्द्धन्-दध्रे हुतभुजि विव-

७. श्वा(स्वा)न्-इव मह: II
[8*]तद्-धाम-निस्सीमम्-अमह्यम्-अन्यैर्-अन्य-ऐव सा काचन दान-शक्ते: I अमानुषं पौरुषम्-आविरासीत्-सल्लक्षणे विश्व-विलक्षणन्-तत् II[9*] खड्ग: श्रीकर[वालत्-आ]धिकं(क)रणं वा(बा)हुर्-महावाहिनी कीर्त्ति:
संभृत-[सू]पकार-विधये पाच्यं सदा दं-

८. शनं I राज्येन्-आपि विना निजोपकरणान्य्-एतानि नि:कंटकं
यत्-सां(सा)म्राज्य-परिच्छदं विरचिरे चिंता-वितान्-ओज्झितं(तम्) II[10*] समर्-आजिर-भाजोऽस्य चिरं निस्त्रिंश एव स: I [खड्गश्-च्-आ]पि धृतो मूर्ध्ना यो जहार्-आसु(शु) जीवितं(तम्) II[11*] [मलय-]वलयस्य्- आन्ते शांते

९. वियत्तटिनी तटे हिमगिरि-गुहागेह-द्वारे दरीम्-अधिनैषधीं I प्रथम-लिखितां सिद्धैर्-यस्य प्रशस्ति-पदावलीं पठति निपुणं स्त्रैणं मोदान्-नभस्थलचारिणां(णाम्) II[12*] कैलास्-आचल-मेखलासु मलय-स्वच्छेषु मेरो:शिरोभागे स्वर्ग्गतरंगिणी-तटभुवि-

१०. स्थानेषु च्-आन्येष्व्-अपि I कृत्वा तर्प्पण-शिल्पजां प्रतिकृतिं वृद्ध-ओपदेशात्-पति-प्राप्त्यै खेचरकन्यकाभिर्-अनिशं यद्-बाहुर्-अभ्यर्च्यते II[13*] एज्यग्व सः पेशलैर्-इष्ट-सिद्धि-प्रा --- पह्वरं स्वं जगद्भिः I गेहे यस्य श्री-विलास्-आभिरामे व्या-

११. गाद्वै तं गीयते चारण्-औधैः II[14*] अमरपुर-पुरंध्री-वं(बं)धुताम्-अव्यलीकां भजति सुकृत-रासौ(शौ) तत्र सल्लक्षण्-आख्ये I प्रतिवपुर्-इव तस्य प्राप्य सद्योऽनवद्यं सुतम्-उदित-विवेकं लोक-कौतूहलं तत् II[15*] अल्हणः प्रणय-पेशलः सतां गर्ज्जतां क्रकच-

१२. कोटिर्-उत्कटः I आनिनाय नय-निन्हवेन यः प्रहृतां प्रकृति-चंचलां श्रियं(यम्) II[16*] लोक्-ओत्तरः स खलु कोऽपि यदा' भिमुख्येऽहंकार-राशिर्-अगलच्-चिर-संभृतोऽपि I संसारि-पाश-भिदु - Uदृशैव यस्य जाताश्लथाः सुकृत दुःकृत कंचुकाश्च II[17*]

१३. पौरुष-प्रतिरंध्र्-ईति पुरंध्र्-ईति च बिभ्यतां I येन लोक्-आनुरुद्ध-आपि प्रतिषिद्धा नग-ओन्नतिः II[18*] तद्-भ्रातृजो जगति **मेघसुतः** श्रुताढ्यः श्रीमान्-अभुद्-अनयचंद्र-पद्-आभिलंघ्य I **गोविंदचंद्र-धरणींद्र गुरु-प्रसादात्-साकेत-मंडल-पतित्वम्-अ-**

१४. लंभि येन II[19*] स(श)श्वत्संगर-रंग-नर्तित-रिपु-स्कंधेन युद्ध-ओद्धुरा वीरास्-तेन न केवलं बलवता ये दुर्म्मदा मोचिताः I अप्य्-उद्दाम-चमु-प्रदान-निरत-स्वान्तेन च्-ऐकान्ततो दूर्-आरूढ-वयस्यता-मदम्-आसौ कल्पद्रमस्य्-आजितः II[20*] टंक्-ओत्खात-वि-

१५. शाल-शैल-शिखर-श्रेणी-शिला-संहति-व्यूहैर्-विष्णुहरेर्-हिरण्य-कलश-श्री-सुन्दरं मन्दिरं I पूर्व्वैर्-अप्य्-अकृतं नृपतिभिर्-येन्-एदम्-इत्य्-अद्भुतं संसार्-आर्णव-शीघ्र-लंघन-लघ्-ऊपायन्-धिया ध्यायता II[21*] गोविन्दचंद्र-क्षितिपाल-राज्य-

१६. स्थैर्याय निस्तंद्र-भुज्-आर्गलस्य I अथ प्रपेदेऽस्य पदं कनीयान्-आयुष्यचंद्रोऽल्हण-सुनुर्-इव II[22*] न साहसांकेन न शूद्रकेण तस्य्-ओपमानं विदधुः कवींद्राः I कृतं भिया यस्य पुरो न कामाद्-अन्येन मन्ये धनुर्-आततज्यं(ज्यम्) II[23*]

१७. उद्दाम-सौध-विबुध्-आलयनीम्-**अयोध्याम्**-अध्यास्य तेन नय-निन्हुत-वैशसेन I साकेत-मंडलम्-अखंडम्-अकारि कूप-वापी-प्रतिश्रय-तडाग-सहश्र(स्र)-मिश्रं II[24*] निद्रा-निरोध-विधयेनिजवल्लभानां हेमाचल्-आमल-शिलातल-तल्प-

१८. लीनाः I कस्तूरिक्-एण-तरुणी-श्रवण-ओपभोग्य-योग्यं जगुः सरस-मग्न-रसो यशोऽस्य II[25*] अविमुक्त-विशालाक्षी ललित्-आनंदिता सदा I कासी(श्-ई)व यस्य देहश्रीः सतां निर्व्वाण-कारणं(णम्) II[26*] अस्थिभ्यो वितरन्-हिरण्यक-

१९. सिपुं संयम्य वा(बा)णं रणे कुर्व्वाणो व(ब)लिराज-वा(बा)हु-दलनं कृत्वा व(ब)हून्-विक्रमान् I **कुर्व्वन्-दुष्ट-दशाननस्य हनन** - - U - - U कः कोऽप्य्-अन्यः स दश्-आधिको U U U - - - U पुण्यो तता II[27*] अद्येह - U नृपते U U

२०. तो निहन्ति पाश्चात्यभीतिमपि भीषणबाहुदंडः I तेजः प्रभावमहतां महसीयमेव पूर्व्वापरा U U U - U U - U - - II[28*] पुण्यैः प्रजानां परिणामवद्भिः ख्याते क्षितौ राज U - U - श्री [I*] आयुष्य[चंद्र] U U -

TRANSLITERATION

1. ... nama: Śivā[ya] (there is space enough in the erased portion for accommodating a verse in a lengthy metre like Śārdūlavikrīḍitam). - - - U U - s-Trivikrama-tanor-ā - U - - U - prāṃśutvena nikharva-ṣo-
2. ḍaśa-samuddeśāṃ-dadhānas-tanuṃ saṃvartta-pramad-oddhata:-kulagiri-grāva-prahāra-kvaṇad-brahmāṇḍaṃ kara-samputena vivu(bu)dhān-madhyo ha - - U - [II 2*] [śrimad]-Bhārggava vi U - U U U - dvaṃso(śo')vataṃso bhuva: I yasmin-rā
3. U U - la-saṅklimir-iva sthāyiny-udañcad-bhuja - - ś-c-opacite parārtha-ghaṭanā vandhy-ānanaṃ jajñire II [3*] te Caṇḍīpati-caṇḍa-tāṇḍava-calac-cūḍā U - - U - brahmāṇḍ-occa-kapāla-randhra-saraṇī-prasthāyi-satkīrttaya: I vīrās-tatra kule janiṃ jagṛhi-
4. re ye Bhārggavīy-āhava-kṣīṇa-kṣatriya-śeṣa-rakṣaṇa-vidhau-(ba)ddho' bhiyogagraha: II [4*] vaṃśyan-tad-eva-kulam-ākulatā- nivṛtti-nirvyūḍham-apratima-[vikrama]-janmabhūmi:I yatr-ātisāhasa-sahaśra(sra)-samiddha-dhāmā Māme'janiṣṭa jagad-iṣṭatam-otta-
5. maśrī: II [5*] mā me dayāstu vapuṣi draviṇeṣu tṛṣṇā niṣṇātir-apy-avirasā sarasendriy-ārthe I ity-udgṛṇann-anudinaṁ sa Dineśavatso mā me pa - U jagade jagadeka[vīra:] II [6*] tad-yuddha-keli-dalit-ākhila-Meda-Bhilla-pallī-sahasra-vanitāsu nikuñjagāsu I utkaṇṭa-

6. kā viṭapino viṭa-viṣṭitāni te sva-staneṣu jaghaneṣu muhur-likhanta: II [7*] purā kīrttyā nyastan-tadanu tanun-ādhyāsitumanā manasvī svarlokaṃ pariṇatim-upe[ty-āti]śayinīṃ sa sarvvasvaṃ kṣatraṃ ka iva bhuvi Sallakṣaṇa-sute śriyā s-ārddhan-dadhre Hutabhuji viva-
7. śvā(svā)n-iva maha: II [8*]
tad-dhāma-nissīmam-amahyam-anyair-any-aiva sā kācana dāna-śakte: I amānuṣaṃ pauruṣama-āvirāsīt-Sallakṣaṇe viśva-vilakṣaṇam-tat II [9*] khaḍga: śrīkara[vālat-ā]dhikaṃ(ka)raṇaṃ vā(bā)hur-mahāvāhinī kīrtti: sambhṛta-[sū]pakāra-vidhaye pācyaṃ sadā daṃ-
8. śanaṃ I rājyen-āpi vinā nijopakaraṇāny-etāni ni: kaṇṭakaṃ yat-sāmrājya-paricchadaṃ viracire cintā-vitān-ojjhitaṃ(tam) II [10*] samar-ājira-bhājo'sya ciraṃ nistriṃśa eva sa: I [khaḍgaś-c-ā]pi dhrto mūrdhnā yo jahār-āsu(śu) jīvitam(tam) II [11*] [Malaya]-valayasy-ānte śānte
9. Viyattaṭinī taṭe Himagiri-guhā-geha-dvāre darīm-adhinaiṣadhīṃ
prathama-likhitāṃ siddhair-yasya praśasti-padāvalīṃ paṭhati nipuṇam straiṇaṃ modān-nabhasthalacāriṇāṃ (ṇām) II [12*]
Kailāsācala-mekhalāsu Malaya-svaccheṣu mero:śirobhāge svargga-taraṅgiṇī-taṭabhuvi-
10. sthāneṣu c-ānyeṣv-api I kṛtvā tarppaṇa-śilpajāṃ pratikṛtiṃ vṛddh-opadeśāt-pati-prāptyai khecarakanyakābhir-aniśaṃ yad-bāhur-abhyarcyate II [13*] ejya-gva sa: peśalair-iṣṭasiddhi-prā - - - pahnaraṃ svaṃ jagadbhi: I gehe yasya śrī-vilās-ābhirāme vyā-
11. gād-vai taṃ gīyate cāraṇ-aughai: II [14*] Amarapura-purandhrī-vandhutāmavyalīkāṃ bhajati sukṛtarāsau tatra sallakṣaṇākhye I prativapuriva tasya prāpya sadyo' navadyaṃ sutamuditavivekaṃ lokakautūhalaṃ tat II [15*] Alhaṇa: praṇaya-peśala: satāṃ garjjatāṃ krakaca-
12. koṭirutkaṭa: I ānindruya nayaninhavena ya: prahṛtāṃ prakṛticañcalāṃ śriyaṃ(yam) II [16*] lokottara: sa khalu ko'pi yadābhimukhye' haṅkārarāśiragalaccirasambhṛto' pi I

saṃsāripāśsabhidu - udṛśaiva yasya jātāślathā: sukṛta du: kṛta kañcukāśca II [17*]

13. pauruṣapratirandhrīti purandhrīti ca bibhyatāṃ I yena lokānuruddhāpi pratiṣiddhā nagonnati: II [18*] tadbhrātṛjo jagati **meghasuta:** śrutāḍhya: śrīmānabhūdanayacandra-padābhilaṅghya: I **govindacandra dharaṇīndra guruprasādāt-sāketamaṇḍalapatitvama-**

14. lambhi yena II [19*] saśvatsaṅgararaṅganartitari puskandhena yuddhoddhurā vīrāstena na kevalaṃ balavatā ye durmmadā mocitā: I apyuddāmacamupradāna niratasvāntena caikāntato dūrāruḍhavayasyatāmadamasau kalpadrumas-yājita: II [20*] ṭaṅkotkhātavi-

15. śālaśailaśikharaśreṇīśilāsaṃhativyūhairviṣṇu harerhiraṇya kalaśaśī sundaraṃ mandiraṃ I pūrvvairapyakṛtaṃ kṛtaṃ nṛpatibhiryenedamityadbhutaṃ saṃsārārṇava-śīghra-laṅghana-laghūpāyan-dhiyā dhyāyatā II [21*] govindacandra-kṣtipāla-rājya-

16. sthairyāya-nistandra-bhujārgalasya I atha prapede'sya padaṃ kanīyān-Āyuṣyacandro'Ihaṇa-sūnur-eva II [22*] na Sāhasāṅkena na śūdrakeṇa tasy-opamānaṃ vidadhu: kavīndrā: I kṛtaṃ bhiyā yasya puro na kāmād-anyena manye dhanur-ātatajyaṃ (m) II [23*]

17. uddāma-saudha-vibudh-ālayanīm-Ayodhyām-adhyāsya tena naya-ninhuta-vaiśayena I Sāketa-maṇḍalam-akhaṇḍam-akāri kūpa-vāpī-pratiśraya-taḍāga-sahaśra (sra) -miśraṃ(śram) II [24*] nidrā-nirodha-vidhaye nija-vallabhānāṃ Hemācala-āmala-śilātala-talpa-

18. līnā: kastūrik-eṇa-taruṇī-śravaṇ-opabhogya-yogaṃ jagu: sarasa-magna-raso yaśo'sya II [25*] avimukta-viśālākṣī lalit-ānanditā sadā I kāsīva yasya dehaśri: satāṃ nirvvāṇa-kāraṇaṃ(ṇam) II [26*] asthibhyo vitaran-Hiraṇyaka-

19. sipuṃ saṃyamya Vā(Bā)ṇaṃ raṇe kurvvāṇo Va(Ba)lirāja-vā(bā)hu-dalanaṃ kṛtvā va(ba)hūn-vikramān I **kurvvan-duṣṭa-Daśānanasya**

hanana - - U - - U ka: ko'py-anya: sa daś-ādhiko U U U - - - U puṇyo tatā II [27*] ady-eha - U nṛpate U U

20. to nihanti pāścātya-bhītim-api bhīṣaṇa-bāhu-daṇḍaṃ:(m) I teja: prabhāva-mahatāṃ mahas-īyam-eva pūrvv-āparā U U U - U U - U - - II [28*] [puṇyai] : prajānāṃ pariṇāmavadbhi: khyāte kṣitau rāja ...... śrī Āyuṣyaca ....

TRANSLATION

Line 1. ... Obeisance to [Lord*] Śiva ....

Lines 1-2, verse 1. [This line is nearly totally erased. But there is enough space for a verse in a lengthy metre such as *Śārdūlavikrīḍitam*]

Lines 1-2, verse 2. ... of the physique of [Lord] Trivikrama ... by His height containing within His body the sixteen doctrines (or *mahā-vidyās*) ..... in Whose palm He holds the universe like (holding) the Moon, whose *kulagiri* (in the case of Bhārata-varṣa, one of the seven great mountain ranges, viz., Mahendra, Malaya, Sahya, Śuktimat, Ṛkṣa, Vindhya and Pāriyātra) whose falling rocks (while striking one another), create noise had, out of wanton arrogance .... .

Lines 2-3, verse 3. The illustrious Bhārgava (i.e., Paraśurāma) ... an ornament of the earth ... like insects ... with firm hands upraised ... having increased, events brought into existence, barren faces ... .

Lines 3-4, verse 4. during the violent dance of the Lord of (the goddess) Caṇḍī (i.e., Lord Śiva), from the rocking head-jewel ... genuine reputations which emanated from the opening in the skull-shaped spherical half of the universe... In that family heroes took their birth, who were determined to resurrect the warrior clan which had been rendered weak by the wars waged by Bhārgava (Paraśurāma) (against them).

Lines 4-5, verse 5. Noble was that very family which was the birth-place of valour which had successfully removed the sufferings of the other (Kṣatriya clans) in which Māme, the abode of thousands of perfect and extremely valorous deeds and who was the utmost favourite of the world.

Lines 5, verse 6. That very Son of the Sun (i.e., Karṇa), Māme, the unequalled hero of the world, uttered everyday the words "may I have no mercy on (my) body, may I not hanker for material wealth, may I be diligently disinterested in sensual temptations ... .

Lines 5-6, verse 7. The thorny trees, like the sensuous villains, repeatedly wrote (i.e., scratched) on the skins of the breasts and hips and loins of the womenfolk of the tribal villages of the plains and hills who had taken refuge in the thickets as a result of the destruction of their abodes in sportive wars waged by him.

Lines 6-7, verse 8. His fame alone having pervaded till then the heavens, the high-minded [Māme], wishing to go to the heavens in person and reside there in that wonderful world, he bequeathed his entire realm along with all the wealth to his son Sallakṣaṇa just as the Sun-god had bequathed all his lustre to the Fire-god.

Line 7, verse 9. As a result of some unknown power of the gift of that realm, which had no bounds and was otherworldly, a super-human valour manifested itself in Sallakṣaṇa; it was indeed an earthly exception.

Lines 7-8, verse 10. The sword was at the tip of his fingers, his hand was verily the great army, his fame, like sumptuously cooked delicacies, were ever palatable; even without a kingdom to rule, these personal instruments enabled him to spread extensively an empire *sans* worries.

Line 8, verse 11. He who was for long intervals enjoying himself on battle-fields, bore on his head his ruthless sword, which was quick to end the lives (of his enemies).

Lines 8-9, verse 12. Within the serene surroundings of the Malaya mountain, on the banks of the heavenly Ganges, at the entrances of the cave-dwellings of the Himalayas, in the caverns in which the hunter-tribes dwell, the accomplished womenfolk gaily sing (literally, read) the strings of his eulogy composed for the first time by the semi-divine beings moving about in the skies.

Lines 10-11, verse 13. On the advice tendered by the elders, in the terrains of the Himalayas, in the pristine pure regions of the Malaya (mountains), in the lands along the banks of the heavenly Ganges as well as in other regions the semi-divine unmarried girls, with intent to gain husbands, ever offer worship to the hands of the satiating images sculpted in his (i.e., Sallakṣaṇa's) likeness.

Lines 10-11, verse 14. He who is to be offered oblations by the beautiful for the realization of their desires ... himself by the world ... in whose abode, which is pleasing with wealth and happiness, hi is sung about by multitudes of celestial singers.

Lines 11-12, verse 15. The people look upon as a phenomenon the fact that, Sallakṣaṇa, who was, through good fortune, enjoying the genuine company of the damsels of the heavens, had happily begotten a son who, by appearance, was no different from his father.

Lines 11-12, verse 16. [That son] Alhaṇa, who was the beloved of the good people is like a pointed saw to the war-mongers. He retrieved the splendour of the habitually fickle-minded Goddess of wealth by means of fair and persuasive means.

Lines 12, verse 17. He was indeed extraordinary and whenever he confronted (his foes the heap of their) arrogance, accumulated over a protracted period, melted away. The garb of good deeds and bad deeds (worn by them) slipped away by his mere looks.

Lines 13, verse 18. He was the destroyer of (his enemies' manliness, and made those who were afraid effeminate; as against the belief among the people, his eminence far dwarfed that of the lofty mountains.

Lines 13-14, verse 19. **His nephew (literally brother's son)**, the widely, celebrated **Meghasuta**, the illustrious one, who superseded Anayacandra; he earned the lordship of **Sāketa-maṇḍala** through the grace of his elder, the lord of the earth, **Govindacandra**.

Line 14, verse 20. Not only did he, who was powerful, put an end to the arrogant warriors who were dancing in unrestrained frenzy in the battles constantly fought by him, but he also gave (to his people) an excellent army which was replete with (soldiers comparable to) the wish-fulfilling trees.

Lines 14-15, verse 21. **By him**, who was meditating in his mind on the easiest means of quickly jumping across the ocean of worldly attachments, **was erected this beautiful temple of [The god] Viṣṇu-Hari**, [on a scale] never before done by the preceding kings, compactly formed [i.e., built] with rows of **large and lofty stones which had been sculpted out**.

Lines 15-16, verse 22. The position of Alhaṇa, whose tireless shoulders were like safety latches for the stability of the king Govindacandra's empire, was subsequently occupied by his younger (son?) **Āyuṣyacandra**.

Line 16, verse 23. Great poets dared not compare him with Sāhasāṅka and Śūdraka; out of sheer fear none save the God of Love dared draw the bow-string in his presence.

Line 17, verse 24. By him, who was of good conduct, and abhorred strife, while residing at **Ayodhyā**, which had towering abodes, intellectuals and temples, **Sāketa-Maṇḍala** was endowed with thousands of wells, reservoirs, alms-houses, tanks.

Lines 17-18, verse 25. The young damsels, who were as attractive as the female musk-deer and does, while they rested on the cool surfaces of the Himalayan rocks, sang about his (i.e., Āyuṣyacandra's) fame.

Line 18, verse 26. Whose bodily splendour, which was ever characterised by glowing eyes, was at all times pleasant with gentle feelings, was a source of salvation for the good just as (the holy pilgrimage centre) Kāśī is.

Lines 18-19, verse 27. Separating [the flesh and blood of the demon] Hiraṇyakaśipu from his skeleton, subduing [the demon] Bāṇa in battle, tearing asunder the arms of the [demon-]king Bali, and performing many valorous deeds, **having killed the evil Ten-headed [demon Rāvaṇa], ...** .

Line 20, verse 29. Because of the subjects' effective acts of merit, the king being famous in the world ... the illustrious Āyuṣyacandra ... .

Bibliography

Banerjee, P., 1986. *Rāma in Indian Literature, Art and Thought.* 2 vols. Delhi: Sandeep Prakashan.

Lal, B.B., 1950. The Painted Grey Ware of the Upper Gangetic Basin: An Approach to the Problems of the Dark Age. *Journal of Royal Asiatic Society, Bengal (Letters)*, Vol. 26, pp. 89-102.

——, 1954-55. Excavations at Hastināpura and other Explorations in the Upper Gaṅgā and Sutlej Basins, *Ancient India*, Nos. 10 & 11, pp. 5-151.

——, 2002 a. The Importance of oral Tradition in Reconstructing India's Past. In C. Margbandhu, A.K. Sharma and R.S. Bisht (eds.) *Purāratna: Emerging Trends in Archaeology, Art, Anthropology, Conservation and History*, Vol. II, pp. 402- 08. Delhi: Agam Kala Prakashan.

——, 2002 b. A Note on the Excavations at Ayodhyā with reference to the Mandir-Masjid Issue. In Robert Layton, Peter G. Stone & Julian Thomas (eds.) *Destruction and Conservation of Cultural Property*, pp. 117-26. London: Routledge Ltd.

——, 2006. Archaeology Vindicates Local Tradition: Bharadvāja Āśrama – A Test Case. In B.R. Mani and S.C. Saran (eds.), *Purābhāratī: Studies in Early Historical Archaeology and Buddhism*, pp. 3-6. Delhi: Sharada Publishing House.

Maharajan, S., 1972. *Kambana.* New Delhi: Sahitya Akkademi.

Mandal, D., 1994. *Ayodhya: Archaeology after Demolition.* Delhi: Orient Longman.

Nair, R.R. and N.H. Hashimi, 1988. Absence of Terraces on a Submerged Carbonate Bank and its Implication to Holocene Sea Level Transgression on the Western Continental Margin of

India. In S.R. Rao (ed.), *Marine Archaeology of Indian Ocean Countries*, pp. 83-86. Dona Paula, Goa: National Institute of Oceanography.

Saran, S.C., 2006. The Northern Black Polished Ware: Origin, Development, Historicity, Dating and the Ethnic Relationship in the Middle Ganga Plain. In B.R. Mani & S.C. Saran (eds.), *Purābhāratī: Studies in Early Historical Archaeology and Buddhism*, pp. 18-31. Delhi: Sharada Publishing House.

Shamasastry, R., 1960 (Sixth Edition). *Kauṭilya's Arthaśāstra*. Mysore: Mysore Printing and Publishing House.

Udayavir Shastri, 1988. *Kauṭalīya Arthaśāstra* (in Hindi). New Delhi: Meharchanda Lachhamanadas Publications.

Virajānanda Daivakarṇi, 2007. *Prāchīna Bhārata men Rāmāyaṇa ke Mandira*. Gurukula, Jhajjar: Harayāṇā Prāntīya Purātattva Saṁgrahālaya.

Zafar Hasan, Maulvi, 1997 (reprint), *Monuments of Delhi*, Mehrauli Zail, Vol. 3.

Index